LAKE FISH

Catfish and Bacon Benedicts (page 39)

LAKE FISH

MODERN COOKING WITH FRESHWATER FISH

KEANE AMDAHL

MINNESOTA HISTORICAL SOCIETY PRESS

 For information, write to the Minnesota Historical Society Press, 345 Kellogg Blvd. W., St. Paul, MN 55102-1906.

www.mnhspress.org

The Minnesota Historical Society Press is a member of the Association of American University Presses.

Manufactured in the United States of America

10 9 8 7 6 5 4 3 2

∞ The paper used in this publication meets the minimum requirements of the American National Standard for Information Sciences—Permanence for Printed Library Materials, ANSI Z39.48-1984.

International Standard Book Number
ISBN: 978-1-68134-028-9 (paper)

Library of Congress Cataloging-in-Publication Data
Names: Amdahl, Keane, author.
Title: Lake fish : modern cooking with freshwater fish / Keane Amdahl.
Description: St. Paul, MN : Historical Society Press, [2017] | Includes index.
Identifiers: LCCN 2016047353 | ISBN 9781681340289 (pbk. : alk. paper)
Subjects: LCSH: Cooking (Fish) | LCGFT: Cookbooks.
Classification: LCC TX747 .A616 2017 | DDC 641.3/92—dc23
LC record available at https://lccn.loc.gov/2016047353

Lake Fish is humbly dedicated to Nathalie, whose patience, support, and care made this book possible.

I'd also like to acknowledge all of the chefs, farmers, educators, and businesses who work tirelessly to make this world a better and more delicious place.

Introduction
- 3 -

CHAPTER 1
BASS
- 13 -

CHAPTER 2
CATFISH
- 33 -

CHAPTER 3
CISCO
- 49 -

CHAPTER 4
CRAPPIE
- 63 -

CHAPTER 5
NORTHERN PIKE
- 75 -

CHAPTER 6
PERCH
- 105 -

CHAPTER 7
SMELT
- 127 -

CHAPTER 8
SUNFISH
- 139 -

CHAPTER 9
TROUT
- 161 -

CHAPTER 10
WALLEYE
- 185 -

CHAPTER 11
WHITEFISH
- 205 -

INDEX
- 219 -

LAKE FISH

Cornmeal-Crusted Catfish with Charred Kale and Tomato, Corn, and Chipotle Salsa (page 40)

INTRODUCTION

KEANE AMDAHL

A DAY ON THE WATER

Some of the fondest food memories I have revolve around freshly caught lake fish. The experience of being out on a boat all day with friends, catching what inevitably becomes our dinner, cleaning the fish and preparing the meal, the final feast—all these memories bring me to a happy place. I was never an avid angler—fishing was always a very casual event for me—but perhaps that's why I've enjoyed it so much. It was never a chore. It wasn't considered work. It was something done on special occasions or on vacation. This lack of expectation kept the task simple and fun, made sitting on the water comfortable, relaxed, blissful. A respite.

I remember many mornings, waking up just before dawn and preparing to hit the lake for the day. Packing coolers and organizing tackle boxes, anticipating some of the fish we might see. Would it be a panfish outing, where we'd wind up with an abundance of sunfish and crappies? Perhaps a largemouth bass or two? Or would it be a day where we'd get lucky and sink into a bounty of larger and more aggressive sport fish like walleye, northern, or muskie? Each fish requires a different tactic, and throughout the day we'd employ an array of fishing methods and tools. Trolling while frantically switching out lures, angling to figure out the day's magic color. Trying to find drop-offs (those cherished "honey holes"), where bigger fish sit and patiently wait for smaller fish to unwittingly swim by. Or just sitting and waiting, trying out different live baits. Any or all of these scenarios could make up the typical fishing day.

Some days we'd unlock the lake's secret right away, but other trips would result in nothing more than a dry live well. The idea was to nab a variety of braggable species, but we were just as happy coming back ashore with a simple boatload of sunnies. To at least have enough fish to facilitate a post-fishing fish fry was the ultimate endgame, even if the fish weren't exactly anything to write home about. In the end, it was more about the time spent with friends than it was about the fish. These memories can't be made in a commercial setting.

A fresh walleye fillet served in a restaurant is never going to be as satisfying as one I've caught and prepared myself—it just can't be. Perhaps that's one reason you don't see lake fish too often on restaurant menus. They're reserved for excursions with friends and family, dining together, sometimes reverently, on something that can be caught locally rather than the kind of fish you have no connection to outside your local grocery store's freezer section. People enjoy catching and preparing fish on their own, re-creating fond memories. For those who grew up in a fishing environment, it's hard to duplicate those feelings of nostalgia in a non-family setting, even though there may be compelling reasons to bring lake fish onto restaurant menus (more on that in a bit).

I define lake fish as recreational sport fish species found in inland lakes, streams, and rivers. Fish that aren't generally caught on a commercial scale and that, with a little patience and know-how, you can catch with a simple hook and worm (if only it were really that easy!). This definition covers a range of species, the smaller-scale fish that have been largely neglected when it comes to large-scale commercial fisheries. In fact, turning to these potentially sustainable fish could help us conserve our oceans. I'm not suggesting that we forgo the local fishing traditions we've created over hundreds of years, but why not embrace these often overlooked species to a greater degree?

We know our commercial food system has yielded a fair number of ecological issues, including many that directly threaten the survival of our cherished lake fish. All across the country, industrial fertilizers used on commercial corn and soy fields get washed into our watersheds. This leads to excess amounts of nitrogen in the water, aiding in the growth of algae, stripping the waters of the oxygen that fish and other aquatic species need to survive. This condition is called hypoxia, and many of our inland waters are directly affected. The kicker is that most of the corn grown in the United States isn't for human consumption. Instead, it goes toward other industrialized uses, such as animal feed, including the kinds of feed used in fish farming efforts around the world. In essence, we're putting our natural resources (lake fish) at risk in order to reproduce them commercially (ocean fish). What if we focused on harvesting natural resources as they are? What if we started to look to lake fish as a potential part of the solution?

Lake fish can often be reared in fairly simple conditions, grow to full market size quickly, and can be managed efficiently—unlike the popular varieties of ocean fish we've come to rely on when we feel like eating "seafood." Before we dig into why we might consider lake fish as a potential alternative to some of the seafood we currently eat, let's examine a few of the concerning issues that exist within today's seafood industry.

SEAFOOD: JUST THE FACTS

Of the fish we eat in the United States, the most common species are shrimp, tuna (typically canned), salmon, tilapia, and Alaskan pollock. More than 90 percent of this seafood comes to us through international imports, usually from unregulated fisheries that rely on a variety of methods that can wreak havoc on sensitive marine habitats, making them uninhabitable for future generations of fish and other animals.

Shrimp sales account for the majority of the seafood sold in the United States, outselling the next two competitors, salmon and canned tuna, combined. But less than 10 percent of that shrimp is caught or harvested domestically. In fact, the bulk of it tends to come from farms in South America or Southeast Asia. These farms are more often than not built upon critically sensitive mangrove forests, which are also home to a variety of highly endangered animal species, like tigers. Our choices at the buffet affect global tiger conservation efforts.

When it comes to domestically raised shrimp, there are some very good, well-managed stocks along the Gulf Coast, where fishers have found ways to cut back on unwanted bycatch, which frequently includes critically endangered sea turtles. There are also reasonably well-managed shrimp stocks in the southern Atlantic Ocean along the East Coast and Gulf of Mexico as well as in the Pacific Ocean off the coasts of California, Oregon, Washington, and Alaska, but sadly much of the shrimp caught in these regions is exported. In fact, more than 80 percent of all the shrimp we eat comes from outside the United States, while we export almost 9 percent of our total annual domestic supply, just over 13,000 metric tons. The overabundance of imported shrimp allows it to be as much as five times cheaper than the domestically caught variety—and our choices as consumers offer a clear example of how we compromise for what costs less and is more convenient, sacrificing flavor, freshness, and sustainability.

Similarly, farm-raised salmon is relatively cheaper and more convenient compared to the wild-caught variety—and also fraught with challenges. Again, our domestic supply comes from well-managed stocks —in this case from Alaska—but is outsourced to other countries. Instead of choosing the wild-caught version, we import farm-raised salmon from places like Canada, Norway, and Chile. Along with these imports come questions about feed stocks, escaped fish and their effects on wild stocks, disease transfer, and antibiotic use.

The majority of us probably don't know where most of the seafood that we eat comes from or the impact that our choices have, but incredible tools exist to help consumers make better decisions, including the free Seafood Watch smartphone app designed by the Monterey Bay Aquarium.

While we currently obsess over the ever-depleting supply of ocean fish, what if we instead turned the tide and started to develop new ideas on how to better utilize our inland lakes, streams, and rivers? What if, instead of consuming imported, questionable seafood, we started to go local like we often try to do with our produce and land-based proteins? What if in the United States we started to look at lake fish as another potential source of commercially viable food? Inland freshwater fish deserve just as much attention as any of their ocean-dwelling cousins: let's expand our seafood platter to include these wonderfully local—and potentially more sustainable—lake fish. As we consider this line of reasoning, a look at the commercial fishing industry's history can help us see how to move into the future.

Local Fisheries: A Brief History

When it comes to our inland freshwater fish species, the diversity in flavor is nothing shy of a food lover's dream. From the mild white flakiness of fresh-caught walleye, perch, and sunfish, to the more robust flavors of northern pike and steelhead trout, to the rich, oily Lake Superior cisco, a veritable pantheon of flavors satiates any palate. Whether pan roasted, sautéed, baked, broiled, poached, grilled, smoked, stewed, or steamed, inland freshwater fish bring a culinary versatility that is thoroughly inspiring.

Along with a laundry list of flavor profiles, inland freshwater fish carry a long and fascinating story rooted in the history of both Native Americans and Euro American immigrants alike. As a cheap and readily available source of protein, fish have played an important role in the diet and everyday life of people throughout North America for millennia.

The history of commercial and recreational fishing varies from state to state, but in the Midwest, more specifically Minnesota, both Native American and Euro and Asian American traditions continue to thrive in tribal and nontribal regions. Freshwater sport fishing represents an almost $2 billion industry in Minnesota, which leads the nation in number of annual recreational fishing licenses sold, and commercial freshwater fisheries take in more than 3.5 million pounds of fish per year. According to statistics from the Minnesota Department of Natural Resources, the state of Minnesota has nearly 160 different fish species within 3.8 million acres of fishing waters. Residents of and visitors to the North Star State are drawn to its waters and their natural bounty, and have been for centuries.

Subsistence fishing has been pursued in the region that became Minnesota for more than 11,000 years. Freshwater fish were at one point so plentiful as to be easily caught, netted, or speared regardless of the season, making fish a substantial cornerstone of many Native American diets, including those of the Dakota and the Ojibwe. Native peoples caught trout, whitefish, and sturgeon using assorted methods: harpoons or hooks fashioned from bone or copper, nets made of birch bark and cast from canoes, and V-shaped dams made of rocks to corral fish in streams.

As the French arrived along the North Shore of Lake Superior in the seventeenth century, native tribes traded fish for various other goods. Much later, Scandinavian immigrants easily adapted to fishing on the great lake, its environment so similar to the seas of their previous home. Commercial fishing in the state of Minnesota dates back to the mid-1800s, and for decades the catches were vast, hitting their peak in 1915 when nearly 10,000 pounds of fish were harvested in Duluth. Unfortunately, the fisheries started to decline in yield due to extensive overfishing. An infestation of invasive sea lamprey from the Atlantic Ocean also decimated fish populations, especially Lake Superior lake trout. Additionally, industrial pollution and runoff from many of the North Shore's budding industries and mining operations contributed to further declines.

Farther west, commercial fishing of Lake of the Woods likely began in the late 1800s, with catches including whitefish and sturgeon and eventually walleye, cisco, northern pike, and burbot (a freshwater cousin to cod). Workers in at least three fish-packing operations cleaned and dressed local fish and processed caviar from sturgeon eggs to be shipped to gourmets around the world. In 1894 the Lake of the Woods fishing industry brought in an estimated 900 tons of fish valued at approximately $75,000, but by 1955, the final year statistics are available, the catch had decreased to just over 500 tons with a value of approximately $86,400.

While the early commercial fisheries depleted fish stocks, the Department of Conservation, founded in 1931 and renamed the Department of Natural Resources in 1971, worked to establish fishing quotas and clean water standards for the state's lakes. During heavy harvesting in the 1960s, approximately fifty licensed commercial fisherman operated in the state of Minnesota; as of 2006, roughly fifty-six commercial fishing licenses were in use. Nearly half of all commercial licenses in the state go to Lake Superior, which has twenty-five licensed fishers operating on an annual basis.

Despite many conservation efforts over the past ninety years, Lake Superior remains in a state of fishery recovery and also faces many new threats. Industrial and terrestrial pollution are key issues when it comes to water quality, and invasive species continue to plague fish stocks. With proper management, however, commercial fishing on the lake has the potential to rebound and could be an important economic driver for the region in the future.

MAKING THE CASE FOR LAKE FISH

While there are currently very few commercial lake fisheries, the potential to develop them is there. Given the sustainability and environmental issues that surround commercial seafood, looking to lake fish is one way to reduce pressures on our oceans. As smaller inland bodies of water, lakes comprise fairly controlled ecosystems. With proper management, they could be developed in much the same way as farms, but without chemical or feed inputs.

A healthy lake contains a variety of fish and plant life. These two factors work together to create an ecosystem within which life flourishes so long as outside influences don't disrupt the balance. The small fish feed on the plant and insect life while the bigger fish feed on the small fish. The plants feed on the dead and decomposing fish, and the cycle continues. Tap into that system in a noninvasive way, and the basic result is a self-sustaining farm.

But wait: if it's so easy, why aren't we doing it now? As it happens, a lot of the pieces that could make this approach a reality are already in place; we just don't think about it in that way, at least not yet.

Using Minnesota as an example, we have only to look to the state motto: "Land of 10,000 Lakes." In fact, Minnesota has more than 15,000 lakes that are ten acres or more in size. Counting bodies of water that exceed two acres or more, there are closer to 22,000. Of those, 5,400 are considered to be fishable. In addition to all of that, more than 18,000 miles of fishable rivers and streams exist within the state, according to Minnesota's Department of Natural Resources.

Taking advantage of these incredibly expansive freshwater resources, a thriving recreational fishing economy results in more than $2 billion in sales annually and is responsible for in excess of 43,000 jobs, according to a 2007 DNR report.

Because of this vibrant economy, Minnesota doesn't look toward expanding its commercial fishing sector, which pales in comparison. Indeed, dedicating waters to commercial fishing could negatively impact the recreational fishing industry. While it's impossible to tell if those fears are warranted, expanding into commercial fishing to work in conjunction with recreational fishing could bolster the overall state economy while providing locally reared food products to millions of Minnesotans. And if done on a national scale, this practice could relieve pressures on certain ocean fisheries.

Speculation with a side of wishful thinking? Sure. But it's something we should stop to consider. In fact, many tools exist to help with these efforts.

For starters, we can look to the success of the pond-raised catfish industry here in the United States. Catfish raised sustainably in ponds provide more than 300 million pounds of processed fish annually, with the total industry worth somewhere around $300 million per year. That's a lot of fish, but the United States consumes nearly 4.8 billion pounds of seafood a year, or roughly 15.8 pounds per person, according to the National Oceanic and Atmospheric Administration.

In California, the pond-raised largemouth bass industry shows the same promise, although at present it basically exists to source the species to regional restaurants. It could, however, continue to grow if demand persists. Most of the bass used to develop recipes in this book was farm sourced, and the quality was exceptional, but because the supply is so low, the cost is largely prohibitive. It's my hope that in the future this industry will expand to a point where the costs come down and the average consumer can have access to this beautiful fish.

Inland lakes could be treated much like farms if only a small number of commercial licenses per lake were allowed. This sort of licensing is done already, but for rough fish, the species people aren't interested in catching, like carp, bullhead, smelt, cisco, whitefish, freshwater drum, and various suckers, very few of which actually get turned into food. Some species are smoked and sold as a local delicacy, but most are either disposed of, ground up and turned into fertilizer, or used for other nonfood-related purposes. By and large the fish we actually enjoy eating (sunfish, crappie, bass, walleye, trout, etc.) are reserved as sport fish for the recreational industry, but with some simple planning and sustainable execution these fish could be utilized commercially while preserving the expansive sport fishing economy.

Currently, the DNR monitors the fish populations of each lake and stocks juveniles raised in various hatcheries to maintain the status quo when the population is not self-sustaining. These can be smaller fish like sunfish or crappies or larger predators like walleye, northern pike, or muskies. The fish are stocked in accordance with each lake's carefully measured biomass—roughly how many fish are presumed to be in the lake at a given point in time. There is a delicate balance to maintain: stocking too many or too few fish can throw the lake's ecosystem out of whack and destroy its health. Fortunately, the DNR puts a lot of time and effort into studying the science of each lake. Similarly, scientifically based management practices used on private lakes or on smaller lakes that aren't popular for recreational fishing could create farms that perfectly mimic the fish's ecosystem and in turn generate a lot of food for a lot of people.

One complicated issue surrounding commercial fishing surprisingly has very little to do with the fishing itself, revolving instead around cleaning and processing the fish. As it stands, much of the ocean fish caught in the United States is sent overseas for processing because it's cheaper to have the work done in countries like China, which means that even the fish caught domestically are first exported to be processed and then reimported into the country. There isn't a lot of infrastructure to support large-scale cleaning and filleting of fish, which is one of the reasons that even locally farm-raised fish can be so expensive. Whereas many view this gap as a challenge, I see it as an opportunity for another locally focused business venture that could provide jobs along with an array of economic benefits that would also allow for expansion not just in the commercial fishing industry but also in sustainable fish farming.

This scenario is not outside the realm of possibility. If we consider alternative methods for acquiring seafood or other cost-effective proteins, we could begin to relieve some of the pressure that's being put on our oceans while building new industries that benefit local economies. And we can establish these commercial fishing industries in ways that comply with strict sustainability standards to ensure the likelihood of enjoying these resources into the future.

USING THIS BOOK EFFECTIVELY

Lake Fish is more than just a niche cooking book. Bring your imagination to the recipes collected here, and you'll be empowered to create a wide variety of dishes with any kind of sustainable seafood.

One of the greatest challenges in cooking with lake fish is sourcing. While developing the recipes in this book, I used a variety of methods to procure my fish. I caught some fish myself; others I purchased online from Canadian fishers. Recently, however, the Monterey Bay Seafood Watch program has given most lake fish from Canada (particularly northern pike) a red, or avoid, rating due to overfishing concerns, so this procurement method might not be the best option at the moment. But it's worth noting that these ratings do change as new methods of management come into place.

Smaller fish species, like sunfish, crappies, and perch, came from the Red Lake Fishery in northern Minnesota. This fishery is currently unrated by Seafood Watch; however, tribal fishers work closely with the Red Lake Nation's Department of Natural Resources to manage the species they fish. As already mentioned, largemouth bass are raised in ponds in California, rated as a "best choice" option by Seafood Watch. I also obtained commercially available fish from Lake Superior, like cisco and whitefish, through my local fishmonger.

While procuring some of the fish featured in this book can take a little bit of effort, the recipes are designed to be easily adaptable to most fish species. Lake fish can be difficult to come by, especially if you're not an avid fisherperson, but that doesn't mean you shouldn't use what's available to you. If you can't get your hands on northern pike or largemouth bass, choose walleye or catfish, both of which are sold at most major markets, instead. If sunfish or crappies aren't at hand, sustainably farm-raised tilapia will yield very similar, delicious results. Instead of smelt, use anchovies. Instead of cisco, use mackerel. Instead of trout (which is generally available), use wild-caught Alaskan salmon. For northern pike, try mahi mahi, a great ocean fish that is both frequently found in grocery stores and often sustainably caught. Let this book be the spark for your imagination.

If you're one of those people who enjoys fishing for sport but hesitates over the chore of cleaning and preparing the fish for cooking, all kinds of great online resources will help guide you through the process. YouTube has an incredible number of videos to instruct on the cleaning of basically any species of fish you can think of. Interested in trying out the northern pike recipes in this book, but don't want to deal with all the bones? A wealth of online videos take you step by step to get boneless fillets. You might not wind up with the prettiest fillets the first few times, but that doesn't mean you can't eat them. After a bit of practice, you'll settle in to a quick and painless process that allows you to enjoy wonderfully fresh fish.

These recipes are also quite flexible. If you spy an ingredient you don't like, substitute with something you do. Improvise and make the dish your own. Leave chiles out for less spice, or add hot sauce for more heat. Swap out spinach for kale or another green vegetable. You're the one who's going to be eating; I won't be offended as you tweak the recipes more to your liking.

Growing up with a fair amount of Julia Child in my life, I appreciated early on that the best way to learn your way around the kitchen is to just go for it. Play with your food; don't be afraid of it. Once you get comfortable with fish, you'll discover that it's one of the easiest and fastest things to cook at home. Make sure your pan is hot and oiled, and you won't have to worry about the fish sticking. Once it's seared properly, the fillet will release from the pan and allow you to flip it over. It'll tell you when it's ready.

Even if a recipe seems complicated, I assure you that the techniques gathered here are all meant to be super simple. Give them a try and you'll come to understand. For example, the idea of pickling something may seem out of reach, but quick pickles are really just that: quick. Boil some vinegar, sugar, and a few other spices and pour the mixture over whatever you're trying to pickle. Let it marinate for at least an hour, and you'll have a really delicious quick pickle to enhance sandwiches, salads, pizzas, eggs, and so much more.

I invite you to use this book to its fullest. Don't get bogged down by the little things. Cook what you like. View recipes as basic guidelines, but then use your imagination to expand on them. As you play around with recipes, cooking becomes so much more fun and making dinner that much less of a hassle.

It's also my hope that this book might introduce you to new flavors from a variety of places. I may have been born and raised in Minnesota, but I love food from around the globe. Most of these recipes are variations on dishes that I regularly make at home, and stretching to embrace other cuisines keeps both the cooking and the eating exciting. Many of the dishes are not properly authentic, but using ingredients available locally helps bring them to life.

So: have fun in the kitchen, mix up your culinary repertoire, and also consider using more sustainable ingredients. Bringing lake fish onto your menus is one way to be more responsible when it comes to buying fish and seafood. The oceans—once thought to be a nearly inexhaustible resource—are showing the effects of overfishing, environmental degradation, and climate change. The only way to bring back our oceans is to change the way we utilize their precious gifts. Science has already proven that fisheries can rebound, sometimes fairly quickly, so long as we change the way we harvest our seafood. These changes range in levels of complexity, but the effort is worth it to continue enjoying our waters' bounty. By incorporating lake fish into our diets, we allow the oceans time to recover and start producing more of the luxury seafood items that we enjoy.

All it takes is a little know-how, and with the wealth of good information that's readily available, it's easier by the day to make better choices as consumers. Think of this book as one of those resources. There's no better way to help save the planet than by eating delicious food. It really can be that simple.

Whole Grilled Bass with Citrus Chimichurri (page 26)

BASS

Bass Spring Rolls

THESE WONDERFULLY FRESH SPRING ROLLS, a healthy and flavorful combination of herbs, fish, and vegetables, would pair really well with either Bass and Mushroom Noodle Soup (page 16) or Crispy Bass and Basil Stir-Fry (page 23). And—bonus—making these spring rolls is probably easier than ordering takeout.

serves 6

1 cup rice wine vinegar
½ cup sugar
2 cups shredded carrots
3 (4- to 6-ounce) skinless bass fillets
2 tablespoons soy sauce
1 (4-ounce) package cellophane noodles
10–12 sheets rice paper
1 cucumber, seeded and cut into ½ by 3-inch pieces
1 bunch Thai (or sweet) basil leaves
1 bunch cilantro leaves
1 bunch mint leaves
4 green onions, greens only, thinly sliced
hoisin or peanut sauce for serving

Preheat oven to broil. Add vinegar and sugar to a small saucepan over medium-high heat and cook, stirring, until sugar completely dissolves. Pour into a glass bowl, stir in carrots, and set aside to marinate for at least 30 minutes.

Slice each bass fillet into 8 equal strips. Grease a baking tray with cooking spray, place bass strips on tray, and drizzle with soy sauce. Broil until the fish is just cooked through, about 3 to 5 minutes, and set aside to cool.

Prepare the cellophane noodles according to package instructions and set aside to cool.

In a skillet large enough to fit the rice paper, heat 2 cups water to just before boiling, then remove from heat and allow to cool slightly. Dip a sheet of rice paper into the warm water to completely submerge; remove from water and lay flat on workspace. At the center of the sheet, layer ¼ cup noodles, 2 strips cucumber, 1–2 tablespoons shredded carrot, 2 leaves Thai basil, 1 tablespoon cilantro, 2 leaves mint, about 1 tablespoon green onion, and 2 strips cooked bass. Wrap as an egg roll or burrito, folding in the sides and rolling up. Repeat until all of the rolls are completed. Serve with a side of your favorite peanut or hoisin sauce.

Bass and Mushroom Noodle Soup

THIS ASIAN-INSPIRED NOODLE SOUP BOASTS incredibly rich flavor, in part because poaching the fish in the broth adds a ton of umami. The soup's complexity is expanded by mushrooms, basil, and jalapeños, making for a really impressive yet incredibly quick dinner.

serves 2–4

- 3 white onions, thinly sliced
- 2 tablespoons sesame oil
- 3 tablespoons soy sauce
- 2 star anise
- 2 cloves garlic, minced
- 1-inch piece fresh ginger, peeled and roughly chopped
- 1 bunch Thai (or sweet) basil, stems and leaves separated
- 1 tablespoon fish sauce
- 1 tablespoon rice wine vinegar
- 4 cups beef, chicken, or vegetable stock
- 1 (14-ounce) package rice noodles
- 2 cups sliced shiitake or portabella mushrooms
- 4 (4- to 6-ounce) skinless bass fillets, cut into one-inch chunks
- 1 jalapeño, thinly sliced

Preheat oven to broil. Place two-thirds of the sliced onions on a baking tray and drizzle with 1 tablespoon sesame oil and 1 tablespoon soy sauce. Broil until onions begin to color and char, about 5 to 10 minutes. Set aside.

In a large saucepan over medium-high heat, stir together the remaining onions, star anise, garlic, ginger, and Thai basil stems along with fish sauce, vinegar, the remaining 2 tablespoons soy sauce, and the remaining 1 tablespoon sesame oil. Cook until the liquids start to reduce and become sticky, then stir in the stock. Bring to a boil and then reduce heat and simmer for approximately 15 minutes.

Prepare rice noodles according to the package instructions. Set aside.

Strain the soup through a colander into a large bowl, discard the solids, and pour the liquid back into the saucepan. Place the saucepan back over medium heat, stir in the mushrooms and broiled onions, and simmer until the mushrooms are just about cooked through, about 10 to 15 minutes. Drop in the bass chunks and poach until cooked through and flaky, about 3 to 4 minutes. Portion rice noodles in bowls and ladle soup just to cover. Garnish with Thai basil leaves and sliced jalapeños.

Bass with Warm Carrot Salad

HERE'S ANOTHER SIMPLE COMBINATION THAT will become a go-to dish—at least I hope it will. This carrot salad, a play on a Moroccan side dish, could go with so many things. The trick is to use a vegetable peeler to slice the carrots into thin, wide "noodles," which helps them cook fast and makes for a really nice presentation.

serves 2–4

- olive oil
- 1 cup raisins
- 1 cup sunflower seeds
- 4 large carrots, peeled into ribbons (see head note)
- ¼ cup harissa paste
- 1 tablespoon sherry vinegar
- 4 (4- to 6-ounce) skinless largemouth bass fillets
- butter
- 3–4 sprigs fresh thyme

Add 2 tablespoons olive oil to a skillet over medium-high heat. Once the oil is shimmering, add in the raisins and cook, stirring, until they begin to soften. Stir in sunflower seeds and gently toast for 1 to 2 minutes. Stir in carrots, harissa, and vinegar, tossing to coat. Remove from heat and set aside.

Pat fish fillets dry and season with salt. Add 2 tablespoons butter and 1 tablespoon olive oil to a large skillet over medium-high heat. When butter has melted and become frothy, add in fillets and fresh thyme. Sear the fish until golden brown, about 2 to 3 minutes. Flip and finish cooking, about 1 minute. Remove from pan and season with fresh cracked pepper. Portion carrot salad onto serving plates and top with fish.

Buffalo Bass with Celery, Blue Cheese, and Bacon Salad

A FUN DISH FOR A dinner party where the guests applaud spicy, playful food. The result looks quite elegant but has all the flavor of everybody's favorite bar food. The celery, blue cheese, and bacon salad might just be one of my new favorite things.

Serves 2–4

8 tablespoons (1 stick) butter
½ cup cayenne-based hot sauce (Frank's RedHot)
1 tablespoon onion powder
1 tablespoon garlic powder
1 ½ teaspoons ground coriander
4 (4- to 6-ounce) skinless bass fillets
4 strips bacon, cut into quarter-inch matchsticks
8 ribs celery with leaves
1 small onion, thinly sliced
2 ounces blue cheese crumbles
1 jalapeño, thinly sliced (optional)
2 tablespoons sherry vinegar
1 tablespoon olive oil

Gently melt butter in a small saucepan over medium heat. Stir in hot sauce, onion powder, garlic powder, and coriander. Remove from heat and set aside to cool. Place fish into a mixing bowl and pour cooled sauce over top. Gently toss to combine, then set aside to marinate for at least 30 minutes.

Place a skillet over medium heat and cook bacon until the fat has rendered and the bacon is crispy, 15 to 20 minutes. Drain bacon on paper towel–lined plate.

Use a vegetable peeler to shave the celery into long, thin strips. Add strips to a mixing bowl along with the celery leaves, onions, bacon, blue cheese crumbles, and jalapeño (if using).

Preheat oven to broil. Grease a baking tray with nonstick spray and gently add the marinated fish fillets, discarding remaining marinade. Broil for about 5 to 7 minutes or until the fish is fully cooked through. Drizzle vegetable mixture with vinegar and olive oil, tossing to coat. Portion the salad onto serving plates and top with fish.

Beer Battered Bass Fish and Chips

FISH AND CHIPS IS ONE of my all-time favorite things, and I've had the pleasure of enjoying this true comfort food in its native countries of both England and Ireland. Here in the Midwest, largemouth bass in a beer-batter crust will bring you really close to the flavor and texture of the traditional cod. And of course you can't have a truly great fish and chips experience without homemade french fries, so I'm including my recipe for super-crisp, perfect fries, er, *chips*. Serve with malt vinegar, tartar sauce, or ketchup.

Serves 2–4

6–8 russet potatoes, peeled and cut into half-inch strips
vegetable oil
2 cups all-purpose flour
2 cups beer
1 ½ teaspoons baking powder
8 (4- to 6-ounce) skinless bass fillets

Place a large pot of water over high heat, bring to a boil, drop in potato strips, and cook for about 5 to 7 minutes or until the potatoes are almost fully cooked but still hold their shape. Remove to a rack or paper towel and drain until fully cooled and dried.

Place another large pot over medium-high heat and fill halfway with vegetable oil. Heat to approximately 300 degrees, then add the fully dried and cooled potatoes. Cook for about 5 to 7 minutes or until fries start to become crisp; they'll still be white and not golden brown at this stage. Remove from oil and drain on a rack or paper towel–lined plate. Reheat oil to at least 350 degrees.

Add 1 cup flour, beer, and baking powder to a mixing bowl, whisking to combine. Stir in a large pinch of salt.

Place the remaining 1 cup flour on a plate. Pat dry the fish fillets and dredge in the flour, then dip into the batter to fully coat. Gently place fillets into the preheated oil and cook for about 5 minutes or until the crust is crispy and golden brown. Remove fish to a rack or paper towel–lined plate. Season with salt. Repeat until all the fillets have been cooked.

Maintain the oil at 350 degrees, then add the cooled fries and cook until golden brown and crispy, about 3 minutes. Remove from oil and drain on paper towel–lined plate. Season with salt. Serve the fish and chips along with your favorite condiments.

Crispy Bass and Basil Stir-Fry

THIS DISH PACKS A HUGE punch in the flavor department. I could easily eat it at least once a week. The onions add great texture to complement the crispy fish, the basil brings both sweet and floral notes, and the jalapeño—if you choose to include it—offers a burst of heat to tie it all together.

Serves 2–4

4 (4- to 6-ounce) skinless bass fillets, cut into one-inch chunks
½ cup cornstarch
vegetable oil
2 large yellow onions, thinly sliced
1 tablespoon freshly grated ginger
2 cloves garlic, finely minced
2 tablespoons soy sauce
1 tablespoon sesame oil
1 tablespoon fish sauce
2 cups Thai (or sweet) basil leaves
1 jalapeño, thinly sliced (optional)
hot cooked white rice

Place bass chunks into a large mixing bowl and sprinkle with cornstarch and a good pinch of salt. Gently toss to coat the fish.

Add approximately ¼ cup vegetable oil to a large skillet over medium-high heat. When the oil is shimmering, work in small batches to gently add in the fish chunks and fry on each side until they just start to turn golden, about 3 to 5 minutes total. Drain on a paper towel–lined plate.

Skillet should have 2 tablespoons hot oil: drain off excess oil or add more as necessary. Add in onions and cook, stirring, until they start to soften and turn translucent. Add in the ginger, garlic, soy sauce, sesame oil, and fish sauce and continue to cook, stirring, until the liquid is almost fully reduced. Add in the basil leaves, the jalapeño (if using), and the fish and toss to fully combine. Cook until the basil leaves have just wilted and the fish is warmed through. Serve with a side of white rice.

Bass au Poivre

THIS PLAY ON THE CLASSIC French dish, steak au poivre, is localized by using beautiful largemouth bass. Traditionally this preparation calls for the steak to be crusted in crushed peppercorns, but to preserve the clean taste of the fish while yielding that essential peppery kick this version adds extra pepper directly to the sauce. This dish also traditionally uses cognac, but a cheap bourbon will do the trick. Serve with sautéed greens; I recommend sautéed spinach.

Serves 2–4

4 (4- to 6-ounce) skinless largemouth bass fillets
olive oil
butter
4 sprigs fresh thyme
fresh cracked pepper
⅓ cup cognac, bourbon, or whiskey
1 cup heavy cream

Pat fish fillets dry and season with salt. Add 1 tablespoon olive oil and 2 tablespoons butter to a large skillet over medium-high heat. Once butter has melted and become frothy, add in fillets and thyme and sear until golden brown, about 2 to 3 minutes. Flip and finish cooking, about 1 minute. Remove from pan and season with fresh cracked pepper.

Remove skillet from heat and add in liquor. Carefully place pan back over the heat and let simmer until reduced by at least half. Stir in cream and freshly cracked pepper and continue to simmer until reduced to desired consistency, about 5 minutes. Either place the fish back in the pan and spoon over the sauce to coat before serving or plate the fish and pour on sauce as desired.

Whole Grilled Bass with Citrus Chimichurri

ONE OF THE BEST, CLASSIC ways to cook fish is to keep it whole, stuff it with herbs and lemon, and throw it on a hot grill. Cooking bone in and skin on sears in the flavor and keeps the fish perfectly moist. This base recipe serves approximately two, but simply toss another fish on the barbie and you've got dinner for four.

Serves 2

zest and juice of 1 orange
2 cloves garlic, finely minced
½ cup chopped cilantro
½ cup chopped parsley
1 tablespoon red chile flakes
3 slices lemon
several sprigs fresh thyme
1 pound whole bass, gutted and scaled
olive oil

Preheat grill. In a small mixing bowl, stir together orange zest and juice, garlic, cilantro, parsley, and chile flakes. Season with salt and pepper and set aside.

Place lemon slices and thyme sprigs directly into the cavity of the fish and coat skin with olive oil. Season with salt and pepper. Place the fish on the grates of a hot grill and cook for 4 to 5 minutes. Flip and cook for 4 to 5 minutes longer. Remove the skin from the fish. The meat should easily pull away from the bones. Serve flaked fish with chimichurri on the side.

Grilled Bass with White Pesto

THIS DISH STARTED OFF AS an experiment. I love pesto as much as the next person, but I also enjoy playing around with the concept and using a variety of vegetables and herbs to see what kinds of flavors I can develop. Here, cauliflower adds an earthiness and the final product lands somewhere between the worlds of pesto and hummus. This delicious sauce could go with so many things, but it happens to pair beautifully with grilled fish. Add a side of your favorite roasted veggies to complete the meal.

Serves 2–4

1 cup finely chopped cauliflower
½ cup freshly grated Parmesan cheese
½ cup toasted pumpkin seeds
2 tablespoons lemon juice
1 cup olive oil
4 (4- to 6-ounce) skinless bass fillets

Add the cauliflower, cheese, pumpkin seeds, and lemon juice to a blender and pulse to combine. Turn the blender to low and gently drizzle in the olive oil until everything is fully combined and loose. Season with salt to taste, then pour into a small container and set aside.

Place a griddle pan over medium-high heat and grease with nonstick spray. Season the fish fillets with salt, and when the pan is hot, gently add the fillets and cook for about 2 to 3 minutes per side. Serve fillets with 1 to 2 tablespoons pesto.

Salt-Crusted Bass with Chive Hollandaise

SALT CRUSTING FISH IS A classic technique that yields incredibly moist, flavorful meat by sealing the fish underneath a dome of salt and letting it steam itself. The amount of salt might seem excessive and a bit wasteful, but cheap salt will work fine. The results really do speak for themselves, and rich, buttery hollandaise is the perfect accompaniment to the succulent bass meat.

Serves 2

1 pound whole bass, gutted and scaled
3 slices lemon
several sprigs fresh thyme
1 small handful parsley
4 cups finely ground kosher salt (see head note)
4 large eggs, whites and yolks separated
8 tablespoons (1 stick) cold butter
2 tablespoons finely minced chives
1 tablespoon fresh lemon juice

Preheat oven to 450 degrees. Stuff the cavity of the fish with lemon, thyme, and parsley. Season the interior with salt and pepper.

In a large mixing bowl, stir together salt and egg whites to a consistency of wet sand. Place a handful of the salt mixture onto a baking tray and create a salt bed just big enough to hold the fish. Place the fish on the salt mixture and spoon the rest of the salt over the fish, using your hands to mold the salt around the fish to completely cover. Bake for 20 to 30 minutes or until the salt crust is golden brown and hard. Poke a thermometer through the crust to check for doneness: 130 to 135 degrees.

Place a saucepan filled one-third of the way with water over medium heat and set a glass mixing bowl on top; the bowl should be big enough to rest inside the pan without touching the water. Add the 4 egg yolks and lemon juice and whisk together. As the water starts to heat the bottom of the bowl, the egg yolks should start to thicken. Whisk constantly until the yolks are thick. Add in the butter 1 tablespoon at a time and whisk continuously until completely incorporated. If the butter is melting too quickly, remove the pan from the heat and allow to cool slightly: if the butter and egg mixture gets too hot, the sauce will separate and break. When all of the butter has been incorporated, stir in the chives. Season with salt and pepper.

Crack the salt crust from around the fish, brushing away any excess salt. Carefully remove and discard the skin. Using a spoon, gently remove the top and bottom fillets; they should pull away from the bones fairly easily. Serve the fillets with a few spoonfuls of hollandaise.

Indian-Style Roasted Catfish with Cucumber Yogurt Sauce (page 46)

CATFISH

Catfish and Chipotle Johnnycakes

JOHNNYCAKES, A QUINTESSENTIAL BUT OFTEN neglected American food tradition, are usually associated with the East Coast, particularly Rhode Island, but are also featured in many modern southern restaurants. This variation, more akin to a dense pancake, can be eaten as a savory snack with salsa and sour cream or, with maple syrup and a fried egg, as part of a tasty breakfast.

Serves 4–6

vegetable oil
1 (6- to 8-ounce) catfish fillet
1 ½ cups milk
2 cups yellow cornmeal
1 cup fresh corn kernels
2 green onions, finely sliced
2–3 chipotles in adobo sauce, finely minced
1 large egg
2 tablespoons butter, melted, plus 1 tablespoon, softened
½ cup all-purpose flour

Place a large skillet over medium-high heat and warm 2 tablespoons vegetable oil until shimmering. Add the catfish fillet and cook for about 3 to 4 minutes on each side or until the fillet is just cooked through and flakes apart easily. Remove from heat and allow to cool, then flake apart and set aside.

Heat milk in a small saucepan until it just comes to a simmer, then remove from heat.

In a large mixing bowl, stir together cornmeal, corn, green onions, chipotles, egg, and 2 tablespoons melted butter. Slowly add in the warm milk in four parts, whisking to incorporate. Whisk in flour 1 tablespoon at a time until consistency is like pancake batter. Gently fold fish into the mix.

Add 1 tablespoon vegetable oil and 1 tablespoon butter to a skillet over medium-high heat. When the butter is melted and frothy, scoop in just under ¼ cup of the batter. Cook until the cake is golden brown on the bottom, 2 to 3 minutes, then flip and cook another 2 to 3 minutes. Remove from pan and repeat with remaining batter. Serve with desired toppings.

Catfish Gumbo

WHENEVER I HAVE CATFISH ON hand, I can't resist making gumbo, a truly American dish that is perfect anytime. While it comes together fairly quickly, the longer you let the roux develop, the more complex the flavor will be. The catfish should be just barely poached, so tender and soft that it nearly dissolves in your mouth.

Serves 4

2 cups sliced andouille sausage
8 tablespoons (1 stick) butter
¼ cup all-purpose flour
1 large onion, roughly chopped
1 green bell pepper, roughly chopped
4 ribs celery, roughly chopped
2 cloves garlic, finely minced
4 cups chicken stock
2 cups sliced okra
1 pound catfish fillets, cut into one-inch cubes
2 tablespoons hot sauce
hot cooked rice
chopped chiles or green onions for garnish (optional)

Cook andouille sausage in a large saucepan over medium-high heat until it begins to brown and caramelize. Remove sausage from pot and set aside. Melt butter and add flour, whisking to a paste. Continue to cook, stirring constantly, until the roux begins to darken. The darker the roux, the better the flavor. Aim for a brick red color, about 20 minutes; the roux should smell nutty. Lower the heat as needed to keep the mixture from burning.

Once the roux reaches the desired color, add back the sausage as well as the onions, bell pepper, celery, and garlic and cook, stirring, until the onions begin to soften. Stir in the stock and okra and bring to a boil. Once the broth has thickened, reduce the heat to a simmer and cook for 15 to 20 minutes. Add in the catfish and hot sauce and poach for 4 to 5 minutes or until just cooked through. Serve with a side of rice and your favorite hot sauce. Garnish with freshly chopped chiles and green onions as desired.

Catfish and Bacon Benedicts

BREAKEAST IS THAT ALL-IMPORTANT MEAL of the day, and there are few breakfast dishes as widely revered as eggs Benedict. This version, wherein catfish fillets are heavily spiced with Old Bay (or a favorite Cajun seasoning) and thick-cut bacon is added to the classic poached eggs and hollandaise sauce, makes a meal fit for a king among kings. Plus, the fish is fried in the bacon fat, so there's that.

Serves 4

8 large eggs plus 4 large egg yolks
2 tablespoons fresh lemon juice
8 tablespoons (1 stick) cold butter, plus 4 tablespoons softened butter
2 tablespoons minced chives
8 strips bacon, halved
2 (6- to 8-ounce) catfish fillets
Old Bay (or Cajun) seasoning
4 English muffins, split

Fill a medium to large saucepan halfway with water, place over medium-high heat, and bring to a simmer. Reduce heat to medium low, gently crack an egg into a small bowl, carefully drop the egg into the hot water (see tip), and cook until the white fully sets around the yolk but the yolk is still runny, 3 to 4 minutes. Set aside and keep warm until needed. Repeat until all 8 eggs are poached.

Over the pot of simmering water, place a glass mixing bowl big enough to sit above the water and add in the egg yolks and lemon juice, whisking to combine. Whisk constantly until the yolks are thick. Add in the cold butter 1 tablespoon at a time, whisking until thoroughly combined, using as much of the cold butter as required to reach desired consistency. Stir in the chives and season with salt to taste. Keep warm.

Place a large skillet over medium-high heat and cook bacon to desired doneness, preferably golden brown and crisp on both sides. Drain bacon on paper towel–lined plate, leaving fat in the skillet. Pat the catfish fillets dry and heavily season with Old Bay or Cajun seasoning. Cook fillets in bacon fat for 3 to 4 minutes per side or until the fish is fully cooked through. Remove from heat and set aside.

Toast English muffins and spread with softened butter. Place 2 pieces bacon, ¼ catfish fillet, and 1 egg on each muffin and drizzle with the hollandaise.

TIP Cracking the egg into the bowl allows you to start fresh if you should happen to break the yolk.

Cornmeal-Crusted Catfish with Charred Kale and Tomato, Corn, and Chipotle Salsa

CORNMEAL-CRUSTED CATFISH IS A SOUTHERN staple for sure, but here it gets a little Tex-Mex spin. Beautiful late-summer tomatoes and sweet corn (or canned/frozen varieties in the winter months) with just a hint of chipotle bring vibrant, fresh flavors to the fish and pair really well with the smoky charred kale. This easy summer dinner comes together in no time. Why not give it a shot?

Serves 2–4

vegetable oil
2 cups roughly chopped fresh tomatoes
1 cup fresh corn kernels
1 small onion, roughly chopped
1–3 chipotles in adobo sauce, finely chopped
juice of 1 lime
1 bunch kale, ribs removed, roughly chopped
1 tablespoon olive oil
1 cup all-purpose flour
2 large eggs, beaten
1 cup yellow cornmeal
4 (6- to 8-ounce) catfish fillets
sour cream for garnish (optional)

Warm 2 tablespoons vegetable oil in a skillet over medium-high heat and add in tomatoes, corn, onions, and chipotles. Cook, stirring, until the tomatoes start to break up, the corn softens, and the onions become translucent. Stir in half of the lime juice and remove from heat. Carefully add mixture to blender and pulse to desired texture (see tip). Return sauce to the pan and keep warm until needed.

Place a large, dry skillet over medium-high heat and add in the kale, gently tossing until the kale starts to wilt, soften, and char on the edges. Add charred kale to a mixing bowl along with olive oil and remaining lime juice, tossing to coat. Season with salt and set aside.

Set up a basic frying station: place flour on one plate, eggs on a second, and cornmeal on a third. Season the flour and cornmeal with salt. Pat the fish fillets dry and dredge in the flour, then the beaten eggs, and then the cornmeal to coat. Place a large skillet over medium-high heat and add in just enough vegetable oil to come about halfway up the fillets. Heat oil to about 350 degrees, then add in the fillets 2 at a time. Cook until golden brown, 3 to 4 minutes, then flip and cook for an additional 3 to 4 minutes. Drain on a paper towel–lined plate. Repeat with remaining fish. Serve the fish with the salsa and the kale and garnish with sour cream if desired.

TIP For a really smooth sauce, run mixture through a sieve and discard solids.

Grilled Catfish with Thai-Inspired Vinaigrette

THIS SIMPLY GRILLED FISH PAIRS with the flavorful Thai vinaigrette in a way that seems almost too easy. It's my favorite way to prepare catfish, and I bet that if you make it once, you'll absolutely be making it again.

Serves 4

1 cup olive oil
⅓ cup rice wine vinegar
2 tablespoons soy sauce
1 tablespoon sesame oil
1 tablespoon fish sauce
1 tablespoon Sriracha
1 tablespoon freshly grated ginger
½ cup chopped fresh herbs (basil, mint, cilantro)
½ cup crushed roasted peanuts
2 green onions, finely minced
1 Fresno chile, finely minced
4 (6- to 8-ounce) catfish fillets
hot cooked jasmine rice

To a mixing bowl, add olive oil, vinegar, soy sauce, sesame oil, fish sauce, Sriracha, ginger, herbs, peanuts, green onions, and chile, whisking to thoroughly combine. Refrigerate until needed.

Place a griddle pan over medium-high heat. Pat the catfish fillets dry and season both sides with salt. When the griddle pan is hot, grease with nonstick spray and gently add the fillets. Cook for 3 to 4 minutes on each side or until the fish is cooked through and flakes easily. Serve with jasmine rice and spoon vinaigrette over the top.

Pecan-Crusted Catfish with Honey Mustard Sauce

PECANS HAVE A SPECIAL WAY of bringing out the flavors in fish. Their earthy, nutty, and slightly sweet nature highlights all of the natural flavors in catfish, and a tangy honey mustard sauce brings in a nice acidic element. Serve with your favorite roasted veggies for a powerhouse of a weeknight meal.

Serves 4

4 (6- to 8-ounce) catfish fillets
Dijon mustard
2 cups finely chopped pecans
1 tablespoon brown sugar
2 tablespoons honey
1 tablespoon cider vinegar

Preheat oven to 425 degrees. Pat the fish fillets dry and season with salt. Coat each fillet with about ½ tablespoon mustard. Add the pecans and brown sugar to a mixing bowl, tossing to coat. Season with salt. Generously sprinkle the fish with the pecans, fully covering each fillet. Grease a baking tray with nonstick spray and gently place the fillets on the tray. Bake until the nuts are golden brown and the fish is fully cooked through, approximately 15 to 20 minutes.

In a mixing bowl, stir together honey, vinegar, and 1 tablespoon mustard. Season with salt. Serve the fish drizzled with honey mustard sauce.

Indian-Style Roasted Catfish with Cucumber Yogurt Sauce

I LOVE INDIAN FOOD, BUT its distinctive flavors are often built on a long list of ingredients that can seem intimidating. Fortunately, this simple recipe utilizes garam masala, a readily available Indian spice blend, to create some kind of tikka masala/tandoori-esque hybrid dish. What it lacks in authenticity, it delivers in bold, delicious taste.

Serves 2–4

3 cups plain yogurt
1 tablespoon tomato paste
2 tablespoons garam masala
1 tablespoon freshly grated ginger
juice of 1 lime
4 (6- to 8-ounce) catfish fillets
¼ cup grated onion, plus 1 small onion, thinly sliced
¼ cup grated cucumber
1 tablespoon Sriracha (optional)
hot cooked jasmine rice
2 tablespoons finely minced cilantro

In a large mixing bowl, stir together 2 cups yogurt, tomato paste, garam masala, ginger, and half of the lime juice. Add in the fish fillets and toss to fully coat. Set aside to marinate for 30 minutes.

In another mixing bowl, stir together the remaining 1 cup yogurt, remaining lime juice, grated onion, grated cucumber, and Sriracha (if using). Season with salt and refrigerate until needed.

Preheat oven to broil. Grease a baking tray with nonstick spray, add the coated fillets, and sprinkle with sliced onion. Broil until the yogurt and onions begin to caramelize and the fish cooks all the way through, about 5 to 10 minutes. Serve fish with jasmine rice, drizzle with the cucumber yogurt sauce, and sprinkle with cilantro.

Soft Scrambled Eggs with Cisco Roe (page 52)

CISCO

Smoked Cisco on Toast

THIS DISH MAKES FOR A simple yet sophisticated light lunch and is jam-packed with flavor. The smokiness of the fish and the creamy-spicy nature of the sauce come together to create a harmonious mouthful of fishy goodness. You could easily substitute any smoked fish for this recipe, but the oiliness of the cisco really makes the dish pop. I like to toast large pieces of baguette to make good lunch-sized open-faced sandwiches, but you could easily turn this recipe into a great party appetizer by cutting smaller rounds and distributing the fish evenly across the desired number of portions.

Serves 2–12

1 tablespoon Dijon mustard
1 tablespoon crème fraîche or sour cream
½ tablespoon finely chopped dill
½ tablespoon sherry vinegar
sliced baguettes cut to your size preference (see head note)
1 large shallot, finely minced
8 ounces smoked cisco, flaked
2 tablespoons finely chopped chives
extra-virgin olive oil

Stir together mustard, crème fraîche, dill, and vinegar in a small bowl. Toast or grill baguette slices until crisp.

Spread the sauce over the toast and sprinkle with raw shallots, distributing them evenly across all portions. Place the flaked cisco on top of the toasts, distributing evenly. Garnish with chives and drizzle lightly with olive oil.

Soft Scrambled Eggs with Cisco Roe

WHEN IT COMES TO LUXURIOUS dishes, soft scrambled eggs tend to take the proverbial cake. There's nothing as elegant as a silken custard of egg with slightly set curd, especially when studded with delicious roe. It's not uncommon to see similar dishes served with top-shelf, expensive caviar, but using roe from Lake Superior cisco is just as classy and a lot more economical.

Serves 2–4

4 large fresh, organic eggs
2 tablespoons heavy cream
butter
2 ounces Lake Superior cisco roe
2 tablespoons finely chopped chives
crème fraîche

Add eggs, cream, and 1 tablespoon butter, chopped, to a large mixing bowl and whisk until thoroughly combined.

Heat a medium saucepan over low heat and add 2 tablespoons butter. When butter melts and starts to froth, add in egg mixture. Using a plastic spatula, continuously fold the egg mixture as the curds begin to come together. If it starts looking more like traditional scrambled eggs than a thick, soft custard, remove from heat and continue to stir, then add back to the stove as needed. About halfway through the cooking process, while the eggs are still partially liquid, add in half of the roe and continue to fold until a luxurious eggy custard forms.

Serve in a small bowl and garnish with chives, a dollop of crème fraîche, and the remaining roe.

Smoked Cisco and Herb Salad

IF YOU EVER FIND YOURSELF in the position of having too many herbs on hand, this salad offers the perfect solution. It's light, but the flavors are full, vibrant, and bright. Paired simply with a basic vinaigrette, it's as easy to prepare as it is delicious to eat.

Serves 2–4

8 ounces smoked cisco, flaked and deboned
1 cup mixed fresh herbs (e.g., dill, parsley, micro-basil, cilantro, chives, and wild picked wood sorrel—but any herb combination will do)
1 tablespoon Dijon mustard
1 tablespoon sherry vinegar
3 tablespoons extra-virgin olive oil
1–2 tablespoons freshly grated lemon zest
1 radish, thinly sliced

In a mixing bowl, toss the flaked fish with the fresh herbs; set aside. To a separate mixing bowl, add mustard, vinegar, and oil and whisk to thoroughly combine. Divide fish and herb mixture among serving plates and garnish with a sprinkle of lemon zest and the radish slices. Lightly drizzle vinaigrette over salad and serve.

Grilled Cisco with Pickled Green Tomato and Pistachio Salad

THIS DISH IS INSPIRED BY a little something I had at a great local Italian spot. The original wasn't served with fish, but the bright flavors of the salad really pair well with strongly flavored cisco, and it's a great way to get rid of any green tomatoes you might still have hanging out in your garden.

Serves 2–4

1 large or 2 small green tomatoes, chopped
1 shallot, chopped
½ cup shelled pistachios, crushed
½ cup cider vinegar
2 tablespoons sugar
½ cup balsamic vinegar
8 skinless cisco fillets
2 tablespoons roughly chopped parsley

In a mixing bowl, stir together tomatoes, shallots, and pistachios.

Stir together cider vinegar, sugar, and a pinch of salt in a saucepan over medium heat and bring to a simmer. Cook until the sugar dissolves; remove from heat and allow to cool. Pour mixture over tomato and shallot mixture and let marinate for at least 30 minutes. Refrigerate until needed.

Add balsamic vinegar to a saucepan over medium-low heat and slowly reduce until the vinegar becomes a syrup. Set aside.

Set a griddle pan over medium-high heat, coat with nonstick spray, and grill fish fillets until two-thirds done, 2 to 3 minutes, then flip and cook for an additional minute to finish. Place the fish on serving plates, top with the tomato and pistachio salad, and drizzle with the balsamic syrup. Garnish with parsley and serve.

Cisco Rice Bowl with Spicy Mayo

IN MY HUMBLE OPINION, THIS might just be the best way to utilize cisco. Resembling something you might see in a Japanese restaurant, this dish usually relies on an oily ocean fish like mackerel, but the cisco really works to bring in all of those great flavors. I like to use a variety of pickled vegetables; marinated cucumbers and pickled onions pair incredibly well with the fish and help cut through the richness of the spicy mayo. Use your favorite method of preparing white rice for this dish, and then pile on the toppings suggested below—or choose a list of your own—to create one of the best flavor experiences you'll ever have.

Serves 2–4

soy sauce
Sriracha
2 tablespoons hoisin sauce
1 tablespoon mirin
1 tablespoon freshly grated ginger
4 cisco fillets
½ cucumber, thinly sliced
rice wine vinegar
sugar
½ red onion, thinly sliced
½ cup red wine vinegar
2 cups white rice
¼ cup mayonnaise
4 large eggs
4 radishes, cut into thin matchsticks
¼ cup chopped cilantro
packaged fried onions or shallots

Stir together ½ cup soy sauce, 2 tablespoons Sriracha, hoisin, mirin, and ginger in a bowl. Add the fish and refrigerate for at least 30 minutes.

Place cucumbers in a nonreactive glass bowl along with ½ cup rice wine vinegar, 1 tablespoon sugar, and a pinch of salt. Let marinate for at least 30 minutes.

Place onions in a nonreactive glass bowl. Bring red wine vinegar, 1 tablespoon sugar, and a pinch of salt to a boil. Pour the mixture over the onions and let marinate for at least 30 minutes.

Prepare white rice following the package instructions.

In another small mixing bowl, stir together mayo, 1 tablespoon Sriracha, 1 tablespoon soy sauce, and 1 teaspoon rice wine vinegar. Refrigerate until needed.

Preheat oven to broil. Drain fish and discard marinade. Place the fillets on a baking tray and broil until skin starts to bubble and char, about 5 minutes. Set aside until final assembly.

Crack the eggs into a preheated greased or nonstick skillet over medium heat. Cook on one side, covered, until the whites set and you have a perfect sunny-side up egg, about 5 minutes.

Place prepared rice into serving bowls and top each dish with a fish fillet, an egg, cucumbers, onions, radishes, cilantro, and fried onions. Add mayo as desired.

Cisco Escabeche with Fennel and Carrot

THIS MINNESOTA TAKE ON A Mediterranean classic packs a tremendous amount of flavor and is delicious lukewarm or chilled. Serve with buttery toast or even as a sandwich filling for a light lunch or dinner. The acidity offers a nice brightness and counterbalance to the rich cisco, and the fennel and carrot help to add substance.

Serves 2–4

butter
4 cisco fillets, cut into thirds, skin scored
3 carrots, chopped
½ fennel bulb, thinly sliced
½ red onion, thinly sliced
4 sprigs fresh thyme
1 cup cider vinegar
1 cup chicken stock
1 small lemon, thinly sliced into rounds

Melt 2 tablespoons butter in a large skillet over medium-high heat and sear fish skin side down until cooked two-thirds through. Remove fish from pan and place in a glass baking dish, skin side up. Add 2 tablespoons butter to the skillet and stir in carrots and a pinch of salt. Cook until carrots start to soften and caramelize. Stir in fennel, onions, thyme, and another pinch of salt and cook until onions start to soften and turn translucent. Stir in vinegar and simmer to reduce by one-third. Stir in stock and reduce by half. Pour mixture over the fish fillets. The heat from the liquid should be enough to poach the fish to completion. Let come to room temperature or chill before serving with lemon rounds.

Blackened Crappie with Red Beans and Rice (page 73)

CRAPPIE

Fried Crappie Pajeon

IF YOU'VE NEVER HAD THE pleasure of pajeon before, you are totally missing out. This Korean-style savory green onion pancake tends to work well as a vessel for seafood. In lieu of the traditional shellfish used for this dish, I like to flash-fry a few crappie fillets and use those. Their beautiful mild texture and flavor pair really well with the green onions and Asian-style dipping sauce.

Serves 2–4

vegetable oil
2 skinless crappie fillets
1 ¼ cups all-purpose flour
1 cup cold water
2 cups (about 2 bunches) green onion, chopped, plus more for garnish
1 large egg
1 tablespoon rice wine vinegar
1 tablespoon soy sauce
1 tablespoon hoisin sauce
1 tablespoon Sriracha
fresh cilantro for garnish (optional)

Add 2 tablespoons vegetable oil to a skillet over medium heat. In a large mixing bowl, toss the crappie fillets with ¼ cup flour, then add them to the skillet and sear until both sides are lightly golden brown, about 1 ½ to 2 minutes per side. Remove from skillet and chop into half-inch pieces. Leave the remaining oil in the skillet and set aside.

In a mixing bowl, combine cold water and remaining 1 cup flour, whisking until smooth. Add in the green onions, the fried fish pieces, and a pinch of salt; using a spatula, fold to combine.

Crack the egg into a small bowl and beat until the yolk and the white are fully combined. Set aside.

In another small bowl, stir together the vinegar, soy sauce, hoisin, and Sriracha. Set aside.

Place the pre-oiled skillet over medium heat. Once hot, pour in the pancake mixture, using the spatula to spread it as thin as you can in the pan, forming it into a round shape. As the pancake begins to set on the bottom, drizzle the beaten egg over the top and cover the skillet until the egg begins to set and the bottom of the pancake is golden brown, about 1 to 1 ½ minutes. Flip the pancake and cook until the other side is also golden brown.

Remove from the pan and let cool 5 minutes. Cut into squares and serve with the dipping sauce. Garnish with additional green onions and cilantro if desired.

Crappie Rachel

THIS MIGHT BE THE PERFECT fish sandwich. It's super simple, it's super delicious, and you'll never want to go back to your generic fast-food fish sandwich again.

Serves 4

2 tablespoons mayonnaise
2 tablespoons ketchup
2 tablespoons sweet pickle relish
4 skinless crappie fillets
1 cup all-purpose flour
1 large egg, beaten
1 cup panko or rye bread crumbs
¼ cup vegetable oil
8 slices rye bread
8 slices Swiss cheese
pickled or braised red cabbage (see tip)
butter

Stir together mayo, ketchup, and sweet pickle relish in a bowl and refrigerate sauce until needed.

Season the fish fillets with salt, coat lightly with flour, dredge in the beaten egg, and coat with bread crumbs. Add vegetable oil to a large skillet over high heat and fry fish until golden brown, about 2 minutes, then flip and cook for an additional minute. Set aside.

Coat one side of the bread slices with sauce and add half a slice of cheese to each. Add pickled or braised red cabbage to 4 of the slices and top with fish. Finish assembling the sandwiches with remaining sauce and cheese-covered slices.

Melt 2 tablespoons butter in a skillet over medium heat and grill the sandwiches until the bread is golden brown and the cheese is melted. Serve with an additional side of dipping sauce.

TIP If you have any leftover braised red cabbage from the schnitzel recipe (page 70), this is a great way to use it. Or you can use premade pickled red cabbage.

Crappie Enchiladas

BY NOW MOST PEOPLE HAVE discovered the joy of fish tacos. I decided to take it one step further and go for the whole enchilada (pun totally intended). I use canned black beans and crushed tomatoes for ease, but if you'd like to use fresh, by all means go for it. My enchilada sauce is homemade, but if you decide to forgo it for your own favorite, I won't be too offended. Serve these enchiladas with your favorite salsa, fresh cilantro, sliced radishes, sliced red onion, and a lime wedge.

Serves 2–4

2 (15-ounce) cans black beans, rinsed and drained
2 cloves garlic, finely chopped
¼ cup finely chopped cilantro stems
juice of ½ lime
1 (15-ounce) can crushed tomatoes
3 chipotles in adobo sauce, finely chopped
1 tablespoon dried oregano
1 teaspoon ground cumin
1 teaspoon ground coriander
8 medium flour (or corn) tortillas
4 skinless crappie fillets, cut into long half-inch strips
1 cup crumbled queso fresco

Preheat oven to 425 degrees. In a saucepan, stir together black beans, garlic, and cilantro stems and cook until completely heated through. Add lime juice and a pinch of salt and remove from heat.

In another saucepan, stir together crushed tomatoes, chipotle, oregano, cumin, coriander, and a pinch of salt and bring to a simmer. Remove from heat.

Spoon 2 tablespoons of black bean mixture in the center of each tortilla and add approximately two strips of fish (about ½ fillet per enchilada). Roll and place in a 9x13-inch glass baking dish. Spoon the sauce over the tortillas and sprinkle on half of the queso fresco. Bake for 20 minutes or until the sauce starts to caramelize and the cheese browns. Remove from oven and garnish with remaining cheese.

Crappie Pie

FOR THIS DISH I LIKE to use small, individually sized ramekins, but you can choose any ovensafe dish, ramekin, or pie tin. The result is a beautifully classic fish pie that's jam-packed with flavor. The creamy interior and the crispy, buttery crust make it a perfect winter dish, but really, it's great for all year round.

Serves 4

butter
vegetable oil
1 medium onion, chopped
2 carrots, chopped
2 ribs celery, chopped
2 large leeks, rinsed well and chopped
2 sprigs fresh thyme
2 cups fish, chicken, or vegetable stock
1 cup heavy cream
4 large crappie fillets, chopped into half-inch pieces
1 sheet puff pastry
1 large egg, beaten

Preheat oven to 425 degrees. Place a large saucepan over medium heat and add 2 tablespoons butter and 2 tablespoons vegetable oil. Once butter is melted, stir in onions and cook until translucent. Stir in the carrots and celery and cook until they become fork tender. Stir in leeks and thyme and cook until the leeks start to wilt and slightly soften. Stir in stock and bring to a simmer. Let simmer until leeks become tender, about 10 to 15 minutes. Stir in cream, cook for an additional 5 minutes, then remove from heat.

Add chopped fish to the pot. The heat from the vegetable base will start lightly poaching the fish. Add the mixture to an ovensafe baking dish or ramekin(s) and top with the puff pastry. Brush the top of the pastry with the egg. Using a small paring knife, poke 3 holes in the top of the pastry to allow air to escape during the baking process. Bake until the pastry is golden brown, about 20 to 30 minutes. Let cool for 5 to 10 minutes before serving.

Crappie Schnitzel, Brown Butter and Bacon Spaetzle, and Braised Red Cabbage

THIS DISH IS GREAT FOR those nights when you're craving German food. The crispy crappie stays moist and flaky, and the buttery and bacony spaetzle is the perfect vehicle for it. The braised red cabbage adds that extra-special German flair and helps to balance out the richness of the dish.

Serves 2–4

6 tablespoons vegetable oil
6 tablespoons butter
1 head red cabbage, sliced
1 cup cider vinegar
1 cup chicken stock
2 tablespoons sugar
2 ½ cups all-purpose flour
2 large eggs
1 cup milk
1 tablespoon Dijon mustard
4 strips bacon, cut into quarter-inch matchsticks
2 sprigs fresh thyme
1 cup rye or panko bread crumbs
4 skinless crappie fillets

Add 2 tablespoons vegetable oil and 2 tablespoons butter to a large stockpot over medium heat. Once the butter melts, add in the cabbage and cook, stirring frequently, until cabbage starts to wilt and soften. Stir in the vinegar, chicken stock, and sugar and simmer until the cabbage becomes tender and the liquid has almost completely evaporated. Season with salt and pepper to taste.

In a mixing bowl, combine 1 ½ cups flour, 1 egg, milk, and mustard and whisk until the mixture looks like a slightly thick pancake batter. Place a medium saucepan filled two-thirds of the way with water over medium-high heat and bring to a boil. Gradually pour the batter into a colander, or some other type of pan with holes in the bottom, and push the batter through with a spatula, allowing the batter to fall into the boiling water in small droplets. When done, the spaetzle will float to the top. Strain and then drain on a paper towel–lined plate.

In a pan over medium-high heat, cook bacon until it starts to turn crispy around the edges. Add in remaining 4 tablespoons butter and continue to cook until the butter starts to turn brown and smells nutty. Add in the fresh thyme and the drained spaetzle, tossing to coat and cooking until the spaetzle is fully reheated. Season with salt and pepper to taste.

In a small bowl, beat remaining egg. Set up a basic frying station: one plate for the remaining cup of flour and one plate for the bread crumbs. Dredge the fish fillets in the flour, then the egg wash, and then the bread crumbs. Add remaining 4 tablespoons vegetable oil to a pan over high heat. Once the oil reaches about 350 degrees, add in the fillets and cook until one side is golden brown, about 2 to 3 minutes, then flip and repeat.

Serve the fish over the spaetzle and top with braised red cabbage.

Pan-Roasted Crappie with Apple-Brussels Hash and Cider Cream

THIS UNIQUE DISH IS PERFECT during the fall season. The apples and the Brussels sprouts pair nicely with the fish, and the cider cream adds acidity and richness. It's also super quick and easy to put together, making for an ideal weeknight meal on the fly.

Serves 4

vegetable oil
butter
4 strips bacon, cut into quarter-inch matchsticks
1 shallot, chopped
8 ounces Brussels sprouts, shredded
1 apple, chopped
2 tablespoons sherry vinegar
4 skinless crappie fillets
2 tablespoons cider vinegar
½ cup apple cider
1 tablespoon Dijon mustard
½ cup heavy cream

Add 2 tablespoons vegetable oil and 2 tablespoons butter to a skillet over medium heat. Once the butter is melted and frothy, add in bacon and cook until it just starts to become golden brown around the edges. Stir in the shallots and cook until just translucent. Add in the Brussels sprouts and apples and cook, stirring occasionally, until the sprouts and apples start to caramelize. Stir in sherry vinegar and cook until fully reduced.

Season fish fillets with salt and pepper. Add 1 tablespoon vegetable oil and 2 tablespoons butter to a pan over medium-high heat. Once the butter is melted and frothy, add in the fillets and cook until golden brown, about 2 minutes. Flip and cook for an additional minute. Drain on a paper towel–lined plate.

Add the cider vinegar to the fish pan and cook, scraping up any browned bits. Once the vinegar has reduced almost completely, stir in the apple cider and mustard, and cook until it reduces by almost two-thirds. Stir in the cream and cook to reduce by more than half.

Serve the fish atop the hash and spoon over the sauce.

Blackened Crappie with Red Beans and Rice

THIS FLAVORFUL SPIN ON A classic New Orleans dish is perfect for any time of the year. Fish stock adds extra depth to the rice and a bit of fresh chorizo kick-starts the beans, allowing for a quicker weeknight version of this southern staple. And never fear: you can fine-tune the blackening spice to your own palate. Make the dish a few times and find your way to Cajun perfection.

Serves 4

2 cups white rice
4 cups fish stock (or water)
3 tablespoons paprika
1 tablespoon cayenne
1 tablespoon onion powder
1 tablespoon garlic powder
1 teaspoon ground thyme
1 teaspoon ground basil
1 teaspoon ground oregano
vegetable oil
8 ounces fresh chorizo
½ white onion, chopped
1 green bell pepper, chopped
1 rib celery, chopped
1 clove garlic, chopped
2 (12-ounce) cans red kidney beans, rinsed and drained
4 large crappie fillets
butter

Prepare rice following the package instructions but substituting fish stock for the water (optional).

In a bowl, stir together all of the spices (paprika through oregano), a pinch of salt, and a few grinds of pepper until evenly distributed.

Heat 2 tablespoons vegetable oil in a saucepan over medium-high heat. When oil is shimmering, add in the chorizo and cook until lightly browned. Stir in the onion and cook until translucent, then stir in the bell pepper, celery, and garlic. Cook until the pepper starts to soften. Stir in the beans along with 1 tablespoon of the spice blend, reduce heat to medium low, and simmer until the beans are soft and creamy in the middle, about 10 to 15 minutes.

Thoroughly dredge the fish fillets through the spice mixture, making sure they're fully coated. Let rest for 5 to 30 minutes.

Add 2 tablespoons butter and 1 tablespoon vegetable oil to a skillet over high heat. Once the butter is melted and frothy, add in the fillets and cook until nearly black, about 2 minutes. Flip and cook for an additional 2 minutes.

Serve the beans over the rice with the fish on the side.

Seared Northern with Mushrooms, Onions, and Beurre Rouge (page 91)

NORTHERN PIKE

Northern Pike Nuggets with Tartar Sauce

A FINE ADULT TAKE ON classic fried chicken nuggets, made special by using northern pike fillets along with a tartar sauce seasoned with cornichons (small French pickles). All too often people don't give northern pike the respect they deserve because their structure makes them more difficult to debone than your average fish, but these days there are many YouTube tutorials to help you through the process. And this recipe is a good choice for when those first few fillets don't come out quite right. Give this fish a chance: the effort truly is worth it.

Serves 2–4

¼ cup mayonnaise
2 tablespoons finely chopped cornichons
2 tablespoons red wine vinegar
1 cup all-purpose flour
1 cup beer (or water)
1 large egg
1 teaspoon baking powder
2 tablespoons Old Bay seasoning
vegetable oil
1 pound skinless northern pike fillets, cut into 1 ½-inch nuggets

Stir together mayo, pickles, and vinegar in a small mixing bowl. Season with salt and pepper and refrigerate until needed.

In a medium mixing bowl, whisk together flour, beer, egg, baking powder, Old Bay, and a generous pinch of salt.

Add about 2 inches vegetable oil to a medium saucepan. Place over medium-high heat and warm to 350 degrees.

Dip fish nuggets into batter, gently place in the oil, and fry until golden brown, about 2 to 4 minutes. Remove from oil and drain on paper towel–lined plate. Season the nuggets with salt as soon as they come out of the fryer. Serve alongside the tartar sauce.

Northern Eggrolls

EVERYBODY LOVES CLASSIC AMERICAN-STYLE CHINESE takeout, and these eggrolls are a delicious play on that winning concept. In fact, they might even be better. The fish stands in for the pork or chicken, and the perfectly seasoned cabbage adds a nice bite. These may be the ideal side dish for those nights when you just want to kick back and hang out at home.

Serves 4–6

vegetable oil
3 cups shredded cabbage (or prepared coleslaw mix)
¼ red onion, thinly sliced
8 ounces skinless northern fillets, finely minced
1 clove garlic, finely minced
1 tablespoon freshly grated ginger
2 tablespoons soy sauce
1 teaspoon sesame oil
8 eggroll wrappers
sweet and sour sauce or hot mustard for serving

Add 2 tablespoons vegetable oil to a skillet over medium-high heat. When the oil is shimmering, add in the cabbage and onions. Once the onions and cabbage begin to soften, stir in the fish, garlic, ginger, soy sauce, and sesame oil. Cook, stirring, until fish is cooked through, about 2 minutes. Season with salt and set aside to cool.

Fill a small bowl with water. Place 2 tablespoons of the cooled mixture in the center of an eggroll wrapper. Dip your finger in the water and wet the edges of the wrapper. Fold by pulling one corner over the mixture and pulling the sides of the wrapper inward, then roll to complete. Repeat with remaining filling. Refrigerate eggrolls for at least 20 minutes.

Place a medium saucepan over medium-high heat. Pour in enough vegetable oil to cover the eggrolls, but do not fill the pot more than halfway. Heat to 350 degrees. Working in batches, add in the eggrolls one at a time and cook until golden brown and crispy, about 3 to 5 minutes. Remove from oil and drain on paper towel–lined plate. Repeat with remaining eggrolls. Serve with your favorite sweet and sour sauce or hot mustard.

Grilled Northern Pike with Fresh Summer Gazpacho

I LOVE THIS DISH NOT only because it's easy but also because it's all about summer. The hot grilled fish nestles in a bowl of ice-cold gazpacho, an amazing contrast in temperature. Fresh herbs accentuate the flavors, and a nice little bit of heat from a serrano chile completes the flavor profile. Give this one a shot, and I guarantee it'll soon be a staple in your summer recipe repertoire.

Serves 2–4

4 tomatoes, cut into eighths
1 onion, cut into eighths
1 serrano chile, cut into thirds
2 tablespoons olive oil
1 cucumber, roughly chopped
2 tablespoons sherry vinegar
juice of ½ lime
4 (6-ounce) skinless northern pike fillets
fresh dill or cilantro

Preheat oven to broil. Line a baking tray with foil and grease with nonstick spray. Place the tomatoes, onions, and chile on the tray, drizzle with olive oil, and season with salt. Broil until the vegetables begin to char, about 10 to 15 minutes. Remove and set aside to cool.

Place the charred vegetables and pan juices in a blender along with cucumber, vinegar, and lime juice and blend until smooth. If desired, strain pulp and seeds from gazpacho for an extra silky and smooth texture. Refrigerate gazpacho until completely chilled.

Pat fish fillets dry and season with salt. Place a griddle pan over medium-high heat. When pan is hot, grease with nonstick spray and add the fillets. Cook on each side for about 2 minutes or until fish is cooked through and flakes apart easily.

Pour the cold gazpacho into a small serving bowl and place the fish in the center. Garnish with fresh dill or cilantro.

Northern BLTs

THE BLT IS ONE OF those classic sandwiches that's fun to play with. It's hard to do better than the original, but the addition of a nice, flaky fish fillet certainly isn't unwelcome—especially one cooked in bacon fat.

Serves 2–4

8 strips bacon
4 (6-ounce) skinless northern fillets
mayonnaise (or Lemon-Tarragon Aioli, see page page 89)
8 slices bread
1 tomato, sliced
lettuce

Place a large skillet over medium-high heat and add bacon. Cook until desired level of crispness, then drain all but 2 tablespoons bacon fat from the pan. Return skillet to stovetop over medium-high heat. Pat fillets dry and season with salt. Sear in the bacon fat for about 2 to 3 minutes on each side or until the fish is cooked through and flaky.

Spread mayo on each slice of bread and top with one fish fillet, two strips bacon, a few tomato slices, and lettuce leaves.

Green Onion and Dill Northern Burgers

EVERYBODY LOVES A GOOD BURGER, but for some reason when it comes to fish, the default seems to be salmon. For a fresh change, dill and green onion add brightness to northern, making an excellent burger for any summertime cookout.

Serves 2–4

½ cup coarsely chopped green onions, green parts only
¼ cup coarsely chopped dill
4 (6-ounce) skinless northern fillets, cut into one-inch cubes
1 large egg
bread crumbs (if needed)
buns
burger fixings: lettuce, tomato, onion, mayonnaise

Place the green onions and dill in a blender and pulse 2 to 3 times to combine. Add in the fish fillets and pulse several times, until the mixture is fully combined and the fish is finely chopped. Spoon mixture into a large mixing bowl and add egg, stirring to thoroughly combine. If the mixture seems wet, slowly add in bread crumbs to soak up the extra moisture until mixture reaches "burger" consistency. Form mixture into 4 to 6 patties and refrigerate for at least 20 minutes.

Place a griddle pan over high heat and grease with nonstick spray. Add the fish patties and cook for about 2 to 3 minutes on each side or until the fish is fully cooked through. Serve on a bun with your favorite burger toppings.

Grilled Northern and Zucchini with Herbed Vinaigrette

THIS DISH TASTES OF SUMMERTIME and works perfectly for dinner party grilling with friends and family. It comes together fast, and the bright flavors are bound to go over well. I chose dill and parsley for this one, but you could use any herbal compilation you like. Basil and tarragon; chives and cilantro; rosemary and thyme? Mix it up and find a combination that works for you. The more herbs, the merrier!

Serves 2–4

½ cup olive oil
2 tablespoons sherry vinegar
2 tablespoons Dijon mustard
2 cups roughly chopped fresh herbs (see head note)
2 zucchini, roughly chopped
4 (6-ounce) skinless northern pike fillets

In a small mixing bowl, whisk together olive oil, vinegar, mustard, and herbs until thoroughly combined. Season with salt and refrigerate until needed.

Place a griddle pan over medium-high heat. When hot, grease with nonstick spray. Add zucchini and cook until charred on all sides, about 3 to 5 minutes. Remove from heat and season with salt. Pat fish fillets dry and season with salt. Grease the griddle pan with more nonstick spray, add the fillets, and cook until just cooked through, about 2 minutes on each side. Serve the fillets with the zucchini and drizzle everything with the vinaigrette.

Pan-Roasted Pike with Roasted Carrots and Honey-Vinegar Glaze

THIS DISH OFFERS UP BIG, sweet flavors that are balanced with a little heat and nuttiness. The flaky, succulent fish pairs well with the carrots' natural sweetness, while slivered almonds, chile flakes, and a little fresh dill help to pull the whole plate together.

Serves 2–4

butter
4 cups roughly chopped carrots
1 cup sliced almonds
¼ cup honey
2 tablespoons sherry vinegar
1 teaspoon red chile flakes
olive oil
4 (6-ounce) skinless northern pike fillets
fresh dill

To a skillet over medium-high heat, add 2 tablespoons butter, a pinch of salt, carrots, and enough water to cover them halfway (1–2 cups, depending on the size of the pan). Bring to a boil and continue to cook until water evaporates, butter starts to brown, and carrots begin to caramelize. Add in the almonds and cook for another 1 to 2 minutes or until the carrots are fork tender. Season with salt.

Stir together honey, vinegar, and chile flakes in a small saucepan over medium-high heat and cook until the sauce just starts to simmer. Remove from heat and set aside.

Place a skillet over medium-high heat and add 1 tablespoon vegetable oil and 2 tablespoons butter. Pat fish fillets dry, season with salt, and, once the butter has fully melted, place fillets in the skillet. Cook on one side while basting with melted butter and oil until the fish is about two-thirds of the way done, about 3 minutes. Flip and finish cooking, about 1 minute. Flip the fish back over and baste with the glaze.

Portion fish and carrots onto serving plates and drizzle with remaining glaze. Garnish with fresh dill.

Grilled Northern with Fried Artichokes and Lemon-Tarragon Aioli

HERE'S A NEW FAVORITE: the bright flavors and a variety of textures are sure to wow anyone at your dinner table. The briny yet crispy artichokes complement the fish, while the aioli brings a cool, creamy, herbal element to the plate. I promise you won't make this one just once.

Serves 2–4

1 cup mayonnaise
juice of 1 lemon
2 tablespoons finely minced fresh tarragon, plus more for garnish
2 (15-ounce) cans small artichoke hearts, rinsed, drained, and halved
¼ cup all-purpose flour
vegetable oil
4 (6-ounce) skinless northern pike fillets

In a small mixing bowl, stir together mayo, lemon juice, and tarragon. Season with salt and pepper and refrigerate until needed.

In a mixing bowl, combine artichoke hearts and flour, tossing to coat. Place a small saucepan over medium-high heat and add just enough oil to cover the artichoke hearts; do not fill pan more than halfway. Heat oil to 350 degrees, then add the artichokes in small batches and fry until golden brown, about 1 to 2 minutes. Drain artichokes on paper towel–lined plate and season with salt.

Place a griddle pan over medium-high heat. Pat fillets dry and season with salt. When the griddle pan is hot, grease with nonstick spray and gently add the fillets. Cook for about 2 minutes on each side or until the fish is cooked through and flaky. Portion fish and artichoke hearts onto serving plates, drizzle on aioli, and garnish with fresh tarragon as desired.

Seared Northern with Mushrooms, Onions, and Beurre Rouge

THIS BOLD AND COMPLEX ENTRÉE was inspired by a slightly different dish I saw legendary chef Eric Ripert make on TV once upon a time. It involves a spin on a classic butter sauce, which to some can seem complicated, but I assure you it's not. You might need to practice a few times, but the worst that can happen is you'll have a broken sauce that still tastes good. The bright, acidic, and silky sauce perfectly complements the fish, while the mushrooms and onions bring an earthiness that rounds the whole thing out. This one is a sure showstopper at any dinner party.

Serves 2–4

1 cup red wine
1 cup red wine vinegar
1 teaspoon black peppercorns
fresh thyme
12 tablespoons (1 ½ sticks) cold butter
olive oil
1 cup frozen pearl onions
1 cup mixed wild mushrooms
4 (6-ounce) skinless northern pike fillets

Stir together wine, vinegar, peppercorns, a sprig of thyme, and a pinch of salt in a small saucepan over medium heat. Simmer, stirring occasionally, until liquid reduces to about 2 tablespoons, 20 to 30 minutes. Remove from heat and stir in 8 tablespoons butter a few tablespoons at a time. The liquid should be hot enough to gently melt the butter. Whisk until butter is fully incorporated into the wine mixture. If the pan gets too cold to melt the butter, return to heat for a minute, then remove from heat and continue. Keep sauce warm.

Add 2 tablespoons butter and 2 tablespoons olive oil to a skillet over medium-high heat. Once the butter has melted, add in onions. Cook until the onions thaw and start to caramelize. Add a sprig of thyme and mushrooms. If the pan becomes too dry, add more olive oil. Cook, stirring, until the mushrooms and onions are thoroughly browned, 10 to 15 minutes. Season with salt and pepper.

To another skillet over medium-high heat, add remaining 2 tablespoons butter and 2 tablespoons olive oil. Pat fillets dry and season with salt. When the butter has melted, add fillets to the pan and cook until golden brown, about 2 to 3 minutes. Flip and cook for an additional 1 to 2 minutes or until fish is just cooked through.

Pour a little sauce on the plate and set the fish on top. Garnish with mushrooms and onions and a few fresh thyme flowers if desired.

Grilled Northern with Romesco Sauce

I'M A SUCKER FOR BOLD Spanish flavors, and this dish absolutely delivers. The sweet roasted red pepper sauce is both rich and light thanks to diced tomatoes and slivered almonds, and it just so happens to pair really well with fish. Serve with a side of sautéed spinach or another sautéed or roasted green vegetable for a great weeknight meal.

Serves 2–4

2 tablespoons olive oil
1 (15-ounce) can diced tomatoes
2 roasted red bell peppers (see tip page <?>)
1 cup slivered almonds
¼ cup sherry
1 tablespoon sherry vinegar
4 (6-ounce) skinless northern pike fillets

Add olive oil to a skillet over medium-high heat. When oil is shimmering, add in tomatoes and red peppers and cook, stirring, until tomatoes start to break down, about 3 to 4 minutes. Stir in almonds and sherry and cook until sherry has evaporated, 4 to 5 minutes. Stir in vinegar and remove from heat. Carefully transfer mixture to a blender and blend until smooth. Season with salt and pepper and set aside.

Place a griddle pan over medium-high heat. Pat fillets dry and season with salt. When griddle pan is hot, grease with nonstick spray, gently add fillets, and cook for about 2 minutes on each side or until the fillets are cooked through and flake easily. Serve fish with a drizzle of sauce.

Grilled Northern with Sauce Vierge

ONE OF THE WORLD'S SIMPLEST combinations, sauce vierge goes so well with fish that after making it once, you'll return to it again and again. Serve with a side of your favorite roasted veggies.

Serves 2–4

- 2 cups tomato cut into quarter-inch cubes
- ½ cup finely minced red onion
- 2 tablespoons capers
- 2 tablespoons freshly grated lemon zest
- 2 tablespoons fresh lemon juice
- ¼ cup finely chopped basil
- 1 cup olive oil
- 4 (6-ounce) skinless northern fillets

In a large mixing bowl, stir together tomatoes, onions, capers, lemon zest, lemon juice, basil, and olive oil. Season with salt and pepper and refrigerate until needed.

Pat fish fillets dry and season with salt. Place a griddle pan over high heat and grease with nonstick spray. Add fillets and cook for about 2 minutes on each side or until the fish is cooked through and flakes easily. Serve the fish with the sauce.

BBQ Northern with Cajun Fried Rice

DON'T LET THE LIST OF ingredients on this one scare you off: most of them go into the sauce, and they're mostly dried herbs and various things you should already have in your pantry. In truth, you could forgo making the sauce and use one of your own favorites, but come on: live a little! This Cajun fried rice is an awesome side dish that goes well with any number of other proteins.

Serves 2–4

olive oil
1 tablespoon tomato paste
2 tablespoons brown sugar
1 (15-ounce) can crushed tomatoes
Worcestershire sauce
2 teaspoons liquid smoke (optional)
2 tablespoons onion powder
1 tablespoon garlic powder
1 tablespoon ground thyme
1 tablespoon dry mustard
1 tablespoon red chile flakes, or to taste
4 (6-ounce) skinless northern fillets
1 cup andouille (or Italian) sausage cut into quarter-inch cubes
½ red onion, roughly chopped
1 rib celery, roughly chopped
½ green bell pepper, roughly chopped
½ red bell pepper, roughly chopped
2 cloves garlic, finely minced
2 cups cooked white rice
2 tablespoons Cajun seasoning

Add 2 tablespoons olive oil to a medium saucepan over medium-high heat. When oil is shimmering, add tomato paste and brown sugar, stirring to dissolve. Stir in crushed tomatoes, 2 tablespoons Worcestershire sauce, liquid smoke (if using), onion powder, garlic powder, thyme, dry mustard, and chile flakes. Bring sauce to a simmer, reduce heat to medium low, and cook for about 15 minutes to let the flavors combine. Season with salt and pepper, remove from heat, and allow to cool.

Pat fillets dry, place in a gallon storage bag or nonreactive dish, and pour in about half of the sauce mixture. Allow to marinate, refrigerated, for at least 1 hour.

Add 2 tablespoons olive oil to a large skillet over medium-high heat. When oil is shimmering, add sausage and cook until the edges start to brown and caramelize. Add onions, celery, and peppers and cook, stirring, until onions start to become translucent. Stir in the garlic and cook for an additional minute. Stir in the rice, Cajun seasoning, and 2 tablespoons Worcestershire sauce and cook until the rice is heated through. If the mixture is too dry, stir in a few tablespoons of water. Remove from heat.

Remove fish from marinade; discard marinade. Place a griddle pan over high heat. When hot, grease with nonstick spray and gently put on the fillets. Cook fillets for 2 to 3 minutes on each side. Serve the fish on top of the fried rice with an additional side of the reserved sauce.

Northern with Pan-Roasted Balsamic Grapes

I RECOGNIZE THAT ON PAPER this dish might come off as a little weird, but it's seriously good, the kind of thing that'll have dinner guests thinking you're some kind of chef-y genius. The grapes take on a robust, rich flavor, the smoky bacon adds the perfect earthy notes, and both magnificently complement the flaky white fish. Serve alongside some roasted greens or broccoli for a truly knockout dish.

Serves 2–4

olive oil
2 strips bacon, cut into quarter-inch matchsticks
2 cups halved red grapes
¼ red onion, thinly sliced
2 tablespoons balsamic vinegar
4 (6-ounce) skinless northern fillets

Add 2 tablespoons olive oil and bacon to a skillet over medium-high heat. Cook until the bacon is crisp. Drain all but 2 tablespoons of the fat from the pan and add in grapes and onions. Cook until the grapes begin to caramelize, 3 to 4 minutes. Stir in the vinegar and cook until the vinegar is fully reduced and the grapes, bacon, and onions are thoroughly coated and sticky. Season with salt and pepper.

Pat the fillets dry and season with salt. Place another skillet over medium-high heat and add 2 tablespoons olive oil. When oil is shimmering, add in the fillets and cook on each side for about 2 to 3 minutes, until the fish is cooked through and flaky. Serve fish along with the grapes.

Grilled Northern with Fennel and Citrus Salad

THIS CLASSIC SALAD REALLY HELPS bring out the flavors in grilled fish. It's so bright, fragrant, and flexible that you may choose to make it all year round. Use fresh or canned citrus based on the season; I recommend oranges and ruby red grapefruit. For fresh citrus, if it's too tart, sprinkle with a little sugar and let it macerate for twenty minutes. For packed citrus in syrup, be sure to drain well, but don't rinse: the sweetness from the syrup will highlight the flavors in the dressing and the fennel and arugula.

Serves 2–4

2 cups citrus segments (see head note)
½ red onion, thinly sliced
1 bulb fennel, cored and thinly sliced, fronds reserved for garnish
2 cups baby arugula
juice of ½ lemon
2 tablespoons olive oil
4 (6-ounce) skinless northern fillets

Place the citrus segments, onions, fennel slices, arugula, lemon juice, and olive oil in a large mixing bowl and toss to combine. Season with salt and set aside.

Pat fish fillets dry and season with salt. Place a griddle pan over high heat and grease with nonstick spray. Add the fillets and cook for about 2 minutes on each side or until the fish is cooked through and flakes easily. Portion the salad onto serving plates and top with fish. Garnish with fennel fronds if so desired.

Grilled Northern with Apple and Green Onion Refried Farro

A HEALTHY ANCIENT GRAIN, farro has a really nice nutty flavor and pairs well with grilled fish and sweet apples, while green onions add a slightly spicy, fresh flavor to this fall-themed dish.

Serves 2–4

2 cups farro
vegetable oil
1 apple, cut into quarter-inch cubes, plus apple slices for garnish
4 green onions, finely sliced
juice of ½ lemon
4 (4- to 6-ounce) skinless northern fillets

Place the farro in a saucepan and add water to cover by one-half inch. Place the pan over medium-high heat and season with salt. Bring to a boil and cook, uncovered, until farro is tender, about 10 to 15 minutes. Drain any excess liquid.

Warm 2 tablespoons vegetable oil in a skillet over medium-high heat. Add apple cubes and cook, stirring, until they start to caramelize, 2 to 3 minutes. Add in 2 tablespoons vegetable oil and the farro. Continue to cook, stirring, until the farro starts to turn golden brown, 3 to 4 minutes. Remove from heat, stir in green onions and lemon juice, and set aside.

Place a griddle pan over medium-high heat. When the pan is hot, grease with nonstick spray and add fish fillets. Cook for 3 to 4 minutes on each side or until the fish is just cooked through. Serve the fish on top of the apple and green onion farro, and garnish with fresh apple slices.

Seared Perch with Caramelized Butternut Squash and Balsamic (page 118)

PERCH

Perch Cocktail

IT'S LIKELY THAT YOU'RE NO stranger to the joys of a good shrimp cocktail. Here's an almost better and distinctly midwestern version. The perch cocktail is both a great party dish and the perfect start to a romantic, homemade dinner. Either way, it's a stunner that's sure to impress your family and friends. It goes really well with a side of tortilla chips.

Serves 2–4

1 cup ketchup
2 heaping tablespoons prepared horseradish
2 tablespoons fresh lemon juice
1 ½ teaspoons freshly ground black pepper
1 tablespoon chopped fresh tarragon
2 cups skinless perch fillets, cut into half-inch cubes
1 cup cubed avocado
1 shallot, finely chopped
1 Fresno chile, finely chopped
fresh cilantro

Combine ketchup, horseradish, 1 tablespoon lemon juice, pepper, and tarragon in a small mixing bowl and whisk until smooth. If it's too spicy, add more ketchup; if it's not spicy enough, add more horseradish. Refrigerate until needed.

Fill a medium saucepan halfway with water, set over medium-high heat, and bring to a simmer. Add in about a tablespoon of salt and the fish. Reduce heat to medium low and gently poach for about 1 ½ minutes or until fish is just cooked through. Drain fish and immediately add to a bowl filled with ice water to stop cooking and to chill.

In a mixing bowl, gently stir together the avocado and the remaining 1 tablespoon of lemon juice. Season with a pinch of salt. Add chilled fish to the avocado along with the minced shallot and sauce. Gently toss everything together to combine.

Serve in one large bowl as a dip or, if you want to get really fancy, in individual martini glasses steakhouse style. Garnish with Fresno chiles and cilantro.

Perch Corndogs with Spicy Rhubarb Ketchup

AS FAR AS I'M CONCERNED, state and county fair season in the Midwest is all about eating as many crispy corndogs as you possibly can, but every once in a while it's nice to mix it up a bit. These perch corndogs take the fair food staple and transform it into something totally new and a thousand percent delicious. Pair them with a spicy rhubarb ketchup and you've got one helluva summertime snack.

Serves 4–6

1 cup cider vinegar
½ cup sugar
2 ½ cups chopped rhubarb
2 tablespoons finely chopped chipotle peppers in adobo sauce
1 cup cornmeal
1 cup all-purpose flour
1 large egg
1 cup buttermilk (or regular milk)
½ teaspoon baking powder
4 cups vegetable oil
12 wooden skewers
12 skinless perch fillets

Add the vinegar and ¼ cup sugar to a small saucepan and place over medium heat. Stir to dissolve sugar, then stir in rhubarb and chipotle and cook until the rhubarb starts to soften and break down, about 10 to 15 minutes. Carefully pour contents into a blender and puree until smooth. Season with salt and pepper to taste. Refrigerate until needed.

Add cornmeal, flour, egg, buttermilk, baking powder, remaining ¼ cup sugar, and a pinch of salt to a large mixing bowl and whisk to combine. The consistency should be like somewhat thick pancake batter. Transfer batter to a large 16-ounce drinking glass for easy dipping.

Add vegetable oil to a medium saucepan and place over medium-high heat. Warm oil to 350 degrees. Skewer the fish and dip into the cornmeal batter. Gently place into the preheated oil and cook until puffed up and golden brown, about 3 to 4 minutes per corndog. Serve on a platter along with the ketchup and your favorite mustard.

Perch Flatbreads

THIS DISH IS SO EASY and also so delicious that it'll become an immediate go-to. It's perfect for lunch, a light snack, or a party with friends. You could also add whatever veggies you want and substitute your favorite flavor of savory cream cheese to shake things up a bit.

Serves 2–4

4 skinless perch fillets
¼ cup onion or garden veggie cream cheese
2 large pieces naan
12 thin slices cucumber
½ cup thinly sliced red onions
¼ cup roughly chopped tomatoes
fresh dill

Place a pot of water over medium-high heat and bring to a simmer. Reduce heat to medium low, add in perch fillets, and poach until cooked through, about 2 minutes. Quickly place the fish in an ice bath and let chill. After the fish is cold, remove from ice bath and flake with your hands. Season with salt and set aside.

Spread the cream cheese on the naan, leaving about a quarter-inch gap along the edges, and then top with the cucumbers, fish, red onions, and tomatoes. Garnish with dill. Slice each piece into eight portions and serve.

Perch Tacos

THESE MIGHT BE MY FAVORITE tacos of all time. The sweet perch is fried crisp in a very simple batter and served with a quick pickled slaw and a spicy chipotle mayo. These tacos couldn't be easier to make, but they also couldn't be more delicious.

Serves 4

- 2 cups shredded cabbage (or prepared coleslaw mix)
- ½ red onion, thinly sliced
- ¼ cup red wine vinegar
- juice of 1 lime, plus wedges for garnish
- 1 tablespoon sugar
- ½ cup mayonnaise
- 2 tablespoons finely minced chipotle peppers in adobo sauce
- 1 cup all-purpose flour
- 1 large egg
- 1 teaspoon baking powder
- 1 cup beer (or water)
- vegetable oil
- 16 skinless perch fillets
- 8 flour tortillas

In a medium mixing bowl, stir together cabbage, onion, vinegar, half the lime juice, sugar, and a heavy pinch of salt. Marinate in the refrigerator at least 30 minutes.

In a small mixing bowl, stir together mayo, chipotles, and remaining lime juice. Season with salt and refrigerate until needed.

In another medium mixing bowl, whisk together flour, egg, baking powder, beer, and a generous pinch of salt.

Pour about 2 inches of vegetable oil in a small pan over medium-high heat and warm to 350 degrees. Dip perch fillets in batter and add to oil. Fry until golden brown, about 2 to 4 minutes. Remove from oil and drain on a paper towel–lined plate. Season with salt as soon as the fillets come out of the fryer. Repeat until all the fillets have been fried.

Place two perch fillets on each tortilla, top with slaw, and drizzle with sauce. Serve with lime wedges.

Broiled Perch with Ramp Salsa Verde and Wild Rice

THIS DISH PILES UP THE true spring flavors of Minnesota and delivers on them in spades. Ramps are wild onions indigenous to various parts of the United States. They pop up for a very short time in the early spring, so you've got to get on them while the getting's good. Their spicy and smooth texture makes for a vibrant salsa that pairs perfectly with any whitefish. In this dish, the ramps help the rich flavor of the wild rice to really pop.

Serves 2–4

1 cup roughly chopped ramps
2 tablespoons cider vinegar
olive oil
1 cup wild rice
3 cups water
½ cup sliced almonds
½ cup dried cherries
2–3 perch fillets per person

Add the ramps to a blender with a tablespoon of the vinegar. Pulse while slowly adding in olive oil, about ½ cup, until salsa reaches desired consistency. Pour into a bowl and refrigerate until needed.

Add wild rice and water to a saucepan over medium-high heat and bring to a boil. Reduce heat to medium low and allow rice to simmer until tender, approximately 45 minutes. Drain rice and set aside.

To the saucepan, add a tablespoon of olive oil and the almonds and toast until they just start to turn golden brown. Add in cherries and cook until they start to soften. Add the rice back to the pot and stir in remaining 1 tablespoon of vinegar. Remove from heat.

Preheat oven to broil. Season fish fillets with salt and pepper and drizzle with olive oil. Broil for about 3 minutes or until the fish is flaky and just cooked through

Serve portions of wild rice and fish and drizzle with salsa verde.

Roasted Perch with Sautéed Radishes and Radish-Top Pesto

THIS SOLID SPRING DISH IS loaded with big, bright flavors. It also makes use of something that most people tend to throw away—radish greens—so it's great in terms of helping reduce overall food waste.

Serves 2–4

2 cups quartered radishes and 2 cups chopped radish greens
zest and juice of ½ lemon
1 cup grated Parmesan cheese
1 cup almonds, toasted
olive oil
butter
1 Fresno chile, finely chopped
2–3 skin-on perch fillets per person

Add the radish greens, lemon juice, Parmesan cheese, and almonds to a blender and pulse to combine. With the blender running, slowly drizzle in the olive oil, about 1 cup, until mixture comes together into a smooth paste. Season with salt and pepper.

Add 2 tablespoons butter and 1 tablespoon olive oil to a skillet over medium-high heat. After butter has melted, add radishes and cook just until they become fork tender and start to caramelize. Remove from heat and stir in the Fresno chile and the lemon zest. Season with salt and pepper.

To another skillet over medium-high heat, add 1 tablespoon butter and 1 tablespoon olive oil. After butter has melted and become frothy, add in perch fillets skin side down. Use a spoon to baste the tops of the fish with the melted butter and oil until the fillets are cooked through, about 2 to 3 minutes.

Place a big spoonful of the pesto on a plate, top with the sautéed radishes and perch fillets, and serve.

Perch with Asparagus Sauce, Roasted Asparagus Tips, and Pickled Shallot

THIS DISH IS NOT DISSIMILAR to a Thai-style green curry, although instead of the traditional curry paste that uses a variety of aromatics and kaffir lime leaves, this version uses fresh Minnesota springtime asparagus. With a side of steamed rice, this simple dish makes a perfect seasonal dinner.

Serves 2–4

¼ cup red wine vinegar
1 tablespoon sugar
2 large shallots, sliced into rings
olive oil
1 bunch asparagus, trimmed, tips set aside, stalks cut into one-inch pieces
1 tablespoon soy sauce
1 tablespoon rice wine vinegar
1 clove garlic, finely minced
1 teaspoon freshly grated ginger
8 ounces coconut milk
2–3 skin-on perch fillets per person
1 Fresno chile, finely minced
¼ cup roughly chopped cilantro
1 lime, cut into small wedges

Bring red wine vinegar and sugar to a boil in a small saucepan, stirring to dissolve sugar. Season with a pinch of salt and pepper. Place shallots in a small bowl and pour the hot pickling liquid over top. Set aside to cool.

Add 2 tablespoons olive oil to a medium saucepan over medium-high heat. Once the oil is shimmering, add in asparagus pieces and cook, stirring, until they start to soften and slightly brown. Stir in soy sauce, rice wine vinegar, garlic, ginger, and coconut milk and simmer until asparagus is cooked all the way through. Carefully pour mixture into a blender and puree until completely smooth. Add sauce back to pan (see tip) and keep warm until needed.

Preheat oven to 425 degrees. Place asparagus tips in an ovensafe pan, drizzle with olive oil, and season with salt and pepper. Roast until the tips start to become crispy, approximately 10 minutes.

Add 2 tablespoons olive oil to a large skillet over medium-high heat. When oil is shimmering, add in fish fillets skin side down and cook for about 1 ½ minutes. Flip and finish on the other side for about 30 to 60 seconds or until fish is cooked through and flaky. Serve the fish by drizzling with sauce and topping with the asparagus tips, pickled shallots, Fresno chiles, fresh cilantro, and a wedge of lime.

TIP Pour the sauce through a sieve to remove any stringy bits left over from the asparagus.

Seared Perch with Caramelized Butternut Squash and Balsamic

THIS RUSTIC RECIPE CAN BE put together in absolutely no time and is a perfect fall or winter crowd pleaser. The squash is jam-packed with bright flavor and just a touch of heat from red chile flakes. The basil and lemon juice bring it all together, while the balsamic offers another layer of acid that adds a tremendous amount of depth to the dish.

Serves 2–4

½ cup balsamic vinegar
butter
olive oil
4 cups butternut squash, peeled and cut into half-inch cubes
½ cup roughly chopped basil
1 tablespoon red chile flakes
1 tablespoon fresh lemon juice
2–3 skin-on perch fillets per person
½ cup toasted sunflower seeds

Add vinegar to a small saucepan over medium-high heat and bring to a boil. Reduce heat and keep at a gentle simmer until vinegar reduces by two-thirds. Remove from heat and set aside.

Add 2 tablespoons butter and 1 tablespoon olive oil to a skillet over medium heat. After butter has melted, add in butternut squash and cook, stirring, until the squash softens and starts to caramelize. Add in basil and chile flakes, tossing to combine. Remove from heat, stir in lemon juice, and set aside.

To another skillet over medium-high heat, add 2 tablespoons butter and 1 tablespoon olive oil. Season fish fillets with salt and pepper and, after the butter has melted, add fillets to the pan skin side down. Cook for about 1 ½ minutes or until the skin is golden and crisp, then flip and cook for an additional 30 to 60 seconds or until the fish is cooked through and flaky. Portion the squash and the fish onto serving plates, drizzle with the balsamic reduction, and garnish with sunflower seeds.

Grilled Perch with Eggplant and Tzatziki

I LOVE THIS DISH. It's got bright, Mediterranean flavors that work well all year round. Serve with some freshly grilled pita bread and you're solid gold. Note that this recipe makes use of "Italian" seasoning—a great shortcut that saves having to measure out a bunch of other dried herbs. Should you not have any premixed on hand, make your own with dried basil, oregano, rosemary, and thyme.

Serves 2–4

8 ounces plain yogurt
2 tablespoons grated cucumber
2 tablespoons grated onion
1 tablespoon chopped basil
juice of ½ lime
2–3 perch fillets per person
2 tablespoons dried Italian seasoning
olive oil
vegetable oil
1 eggplant, cut into strips
1 shallot, finely minced
1 clove garlic, finely minced
1 roasted red bell pepper, cut into half-inch pieces (see tip page <?>)
1 tablespoon balsamic vinegar
2 tablespoons finely chopped fresh mint
2 tablespoons fresh tarragon leaves
grilled pita wedges

Stir together yogurt, grated cucumber, grated onion, basil, and lime juice in a mixing bowl. Season with salt and pepper and refrigerate until needed.

Add fish fillets to a plastic bag with Italian seasoning and about 2 tablespoons olive oil. Set aside to marinate for 20 to 30 minutes.

Set a grill pan over high heat and brush generously with vegetable oil. Quickly brown the eggplant strips on both sides and remove. When cool enough to handle, cut the strips into 1- to 2-inch pieces and set aside.

Add 1 tablespoon olive oil to a skillet over medium-high heat. When oil is shimmering, add the shallot. Cook, stirring, until shallot begins to soften, then add in garlic, roasted red pepper, and eggplant. Cook until the eggplant and roasted red pepper are warmed through. Add vinegar to the pan and cook, scraping up any browned bits. After the vinegar is completely reduced, stir in fresh mint and tarragon and remove from heat. Season with salt and pepper to taste.

Remove the fish from the plastic bag and season with salt. Add the fillets, skin side down, to the grill pan over high heat. Cook until the fish is about two-thirds done and the skin is crispy with good grill marks, about 1 ½ to 2 minutes. Flip and cook an additional 30 seconds, then remove from heat. Divide the eggplant mixture and fish onto serving plates and drizzle with the tzatziki sauce. Serve with grilled pita wedges.

Grilled Perch with Cucumber Mignonette

A MIGNONETTE IS A SIMPLE, vinegar-based sauce often served alongside raw oysters. Its brightness is an amazing complement to grilled fish, especially on hot summer days. This version makes use of cucumbers and Fresno chiles to ramp it up a bit. Serve with a bounty of grilled summer veggies.

Serves 2–4

¼ cup finely minced cucumber
1 Fresno chile, finely minced
1 small shallot, finely minced
½ cup sherry vinegar
1 tablespoon sugar
vegetable oil
2–4 skin-on perch fillets per person
fresh cilantro

Add cucumber, chile, shallot, vinegar, and sugar to a small mixing bowl, stirring to combine. Season with salt and refrigerate at least 30 minutes.

Place a grill pan over high heat and grease with about 1 tablespoon vegetable oil, or oil a grill grate set over hot coals. Once the grill pan is really hot, season the fish with salt and add the fillets skin side down, pressing to flatten. Cook until the fish is nearly done, about 2 to 2 ½ minutes, then flip and finish cooking on the other side, about 30 seconds. Place the grilled fish on a serving platter, drizzle with the mignonette, and garnish with cilantro.

Grilled Perch with Mushroom Broth and Fiddlehead Ferns

THIS FUN AND DELICIOUS DISH makes use of an often neglected ingredient: dried mushrooms. Dried mushrooms can be fairly inexpensive, and a little goes a long way. The liquid made from rehydrating them is basically flavor gold, and harnessing it is one of the best favors you can do for yourself. Fiddlehead ferns are a delicious, hyper-seasonal springtime ingredient. Find them at specialty stores, co-ops, or farmers markets. Their flavor is similar to asparagus, which is a worthy substitute.

Serves 2–4

8 ounces fiddlehead ferns, or substitute asparagus
1 ½ ounces dried mushrooms, preferably a wild mix
butter
1 small shallot, finely minced
2 tablespoons finely minced celery
2 tablespoons finely minced carrot
vegetable oil
2–4 skin-on perch fillets per person
1 teaspoon red chile flakes

Add 2 cups water to a small or medium saucepan and bring to a simmer over medium-high heat. Add in the fiddleheads and simmer for 5 minutes. Lift fiddleheads out with a slotted spoon and drain on a paper towel–lined plate. Remove pan from heat, stir in the mushrooms, and let them steep, covered, for about 10 minutes. Lift the mushrooms out with a slotted spoon. Strain the liquid through a coffee filter into a bowl to remove any grit; reserve the liquid.

Add 2 tablespoons butter to the saucepan and place it back over medium-high heat. After the butter has melted, add in shallots, celery, and carrots and cook, stirring, until the vegetables start to soften. Add in the mushrooms and their liquid and reduce heat to low, simmering until the stock reduces by at least half. Add in another tablespoon of butter, season with salt and pepper, and keep warm over low heat until needed.

Place a grill pan over high heat and grease with vegetable oil. Season the perch with salt and place the fillets skin side down on the pan. Cook until the fish is nearly done, about 2 to 2 ½ minutes, then flip and cook for an additional 30 seconds. Remove from heat. Add the fiddlehead ferns to the grill pan, season with salt, and sprinkle on chile flakes. Cook for about 2 minutes on each side.

Portion the fish and fiddleheads onto serving plates, top with mushroom and vegetable mixture, and drizzle remaining broth over the fish.

Smelt in Sofrito (page 132)

SMELT

Harissa Grilled Smelt with Mint and Cilantro Yogurt

THIS GREAT SUMMER DISH HAS got heat coupled with that beautifully smoky grill flavor. The yogurt sauce helps to dial some of that back by offering cool and refreshing undertones. I like to skewer the smelt to prevent them from falling through the grill grates, but if you're using a griddle pan on the stovetop, this step is not necessary.

Serves 2–4

1 pound cleaned smelt
¼ cup harissa paste
8 ounces plain yogurt
1 tablespoon chopped mint
1 tablespoon chopped cilantro
1 tablespoon grated onion
juice of ½ lime
wooden skewers

Add the smelt and harissa paste to a large mixing bowl and stir to coat. Let marinate for at least 2 hours or overnight. For the sauce, stir together the yogurt, mint, cilantro, onion, and lime juice. Season with salt to taste and refrigerate until needed.

Skewer the smelt and place on a well-oiled grill over medium-high heat. Cook about 1 to 2 minutes per side. Place the smelt skewers on a platter with a side of the dipping sauce and go to town.

Tempura Smelt with Asian-Style Dipping Sauce

A REALLY GREAT WAY TO use smelt. Nicely fried in a light, crispy batter, they pair well with this flavorful, spicy sauce. Here's a dish that's guaranteed to go quickly.

Serves 2–4

1 tablespoon finely minced garlic
1 tablespoon freshly grated ginger
1 tablespoon chopped green onion greens
2 tablespoons soy sauce
2 tablespoons hoisin sauce
2 tablespoons rice wine vinegar
1–2 tablespoons Sriracha, to taste
1 cup all-purpose flour
1 ½–2 cups cold sparkling water
2–3 cups vegetable oil
1 pound cleaned smelt

Stir together garlic, ginger, green onion, soy sauce, hoisin sauce, vinegar, and Sriracha in a small mixing bowl. Refrigerate until needed.

In a large mixing bowl, stir together flour and sparkling water. The batter should be fairly thin, making small ribbons when drizzled from a spoon.

Add oil to a medium or large saucepan, making sure not to fill more than halfway, and set over medium-high heat. Heat the oil to 350 degrees.

Working in batches, dredge smelt in the batter and then place in the oil. Cook until the smelt turns golden brown, about 2 to 3 minutes, then drain on a paper towel–lined plate. Season with salt. Place smelt in a serving bowl and serve with a side of the dipping sauce.

Smelt in Sofrito

THIS DISH IS IN THE style of Spanish tapas, small plates meant for sharing and snacking—perfect for a themed dinner party. Traditionally made with Spanish boquerones (anchovies), it works really well with Lake Superior smelt. Serve alongside a nice Spanish red wine for a fine fiesta.

Serves 2–8

1 pound cleaned smelt
olive oil
1 large yellow onion, sliced
1 large green pepper, sliced
1 roasted red bell pepper, sliced (see tip page <?>)
1 tablespoon tomato paste
1 clove garlic, finely minced
2 tablespoons Spanish or smoked paprika
1 teaspoon cayenne
¼ cup sherry
lime wedges for serving
fresh cilantro

Add the smelt to a mixing bowl, drizzle with olive oil, and season with salt. Set a griddle pan over medium-high heat, add the smelt, and grill until they begin to char on both sides. Remove from heat and set aside.

Warm 2 tablespoons olive oil in a large skillet over medium-high heat and add onion, green pepper, and red pepper and cook, stirring, until the onions begin to become translucent and the peppers begin to soften. Stir in tomato paste and garlic to coat the vegetables, then stir in paprika and cayenne and continue to cook until the mixture starts to caramelize, about 3 minutes. Pour in the sherry and cook, scraping up any browned bits, until nearly reduced. Add in the smelt, tossing to coat. Serve on a platter along with a few lime wedges and cilantro sprigs if desired.

Pan-Fried Smelt with Garlic Chips, Lemon, Parsley, and Olive Oil

THIS CLASSIC DISH COULD BE served tapas style for a dinner party or as a full entrée with a simple salad of fresh greens. No matter how you cut it, these crispy little smelt pop with big flavors from the fried garlic chips, fresh lemon juice, herbaceous parsley, and peppery olive oil.

Serves 2–4

1 pound cleaned smelt
½ cup all-purpose flour
¼ cup vegetable oil
2 cloves garlic, thinly sliced
¼ cup finely chopped parsley
1 lemon, cut into 8 wedges
good quality olive oil

Place the smelt in a large mixing bowl, sprinkle with flour, season with salt, and toss to coat. Set aside.

Add vegetable oil to a large skillet over medium-high heat. When oil is shimmering, work in batches to cook the smelt until golden brown and crisp, about 2 minutes per side. Drain on a paper towel–lined plate. Repeat until all of the smelt are cooked.

Add garlic to the hot oil and cook until chips are golden brown and crisp, about 1 minute. Drain garlic chips on a paper towel–lined plate.

Place the cooked smelt in a mixing bowl and add the parsley and garlic chips. Season with salt and toss to coat. Serve the smelt with lemon wedges and lightly drizzle with olive oil.

Grilled Smelt Caesar Salad

A PRIMARY INGREDIENT IN A traditional Caesar salad is the anchovy, but here grilled smelt works beautifully. If you're a Caesar fan, give this freshwater version a try.

Serves 4

½ pound cleaned smelt
olive oil
3 large egg yolks
1 tablespoon mustard
¼ cup freshly grated Parmesan cheese, plus more for serving
juice of ½ lemon
1 teaspoon Worcestershire sauce
2 romaine hearts, halved
croutons

Add the smelt to a mixing bowl, drizzle with olive oil, and season with salt. Set a griddle pan over medium-high heat, add the smelt, and grill on one side for 1 ½ to 2 minutes, then flip and grill for an additional 1 ½ to 2 minutes, until fully cooked. Remove from heat and set aside.

Add 6 of the grilled smelt to a blender along with egg yolks, mustard, Parmesan cheese, lemon juice, and Worcestershire sauce and pulse to combine. With the blender running on low, slowly drizzle in about 1 ½ cups olive oil until dressing reaches desired consistency, which should coat a spoon.

Set griddle pan back over medium-high heat. Spray the cut sides of the romaine with nonstick spray and season with salt. Cook until the leaves just begin to char, 1 to 1 ½ minutes. Set romaine hearts on serving plates, drizzle with dressing, and top with remaining smelt, additional cheese, and croutons.

Sunfish Paella
(page 150)

SUNFISH

Sunfish Pot Stickers

THERE'S SOMETHING ABOUT POT STICKERS. **Maybe it's the texture, the blend of well-balanced Asian flavors, or the fact that they come in a lot of different varieties. Whatever it is, I just cannot get enough of them. Fortunately, this recipe not only is simple but also makes a ton (about thirty, depending on wrapper size)—perfect for any party.**

Serves 4+

8 ounces skinless sunfish fillets, finely minced
2 tablespoons finely minced red onion
1 green onion, white and green parts, finely minced
1 Fresno chile, finely minced
1 tablespoon finely minced cilantro
1 tablespoon soy sauce
1 tablespoon fresh lime juice
1 tablespoon freshly grated ginger
1 tablespoon finely minced garlic
about 30 won ton wrappers
olive oil
soy sauce

Add sunfish, red and green onions, chile, cilantro, soy sauce, lime juice, ginger, garlic, and a pinch of salt to a medium mixing bowl and stir to combine. Mixture should be lightly dressed but not overly wet.

Fill a small bowl with water. Place one won ton wrapper on a large cutting board or work space. Dip your finger in the bowl of water and run your wet finger around the edges of the wrapper. Place about 1 teaspoon of filling in the middle of the wrapper and fold over to make a half moon, pressing the edges together to seal them tight. Repeat with remaining filling and wrappers.

Add 2 tablespoons olive oil to a large skillet over medium-high heat. Once the oil is shimmering, work in batches to add pot stickers and sear one side golden brown, about 1 to 2 minutes. Remove from pan and set aside, continuing to work in batches until the rest of the pot stickers are done. Add more oil if needed.

Drain most of the oil from the pan. Add in 1 batch of pot stickers, seared side down, and then add about ¼ to ½ cup water, to a depth of ⅛ inch: do not cover the pot stickers with water. Cover the skillet to steam the pot stickers for 1 to 1 ½ minutes or until filling is heated through. Remove and repeat with the rest of the pot stickers, adding more water as needed. Serve with soy sauce.

Sunfish Sandwich

FORGET TUNA FISH, FRIENDS, BECAUSE this sandwich puts that dry tinned fish to shame. Don't get me wrong: I love responsibly sourced canned tuna, but this alternative makes a really delicious sandwich perfect for a summertime picnic lunch. The fish is gently poached and then chilled before it gets turned into a classic fish salad sandwich. Do it up right with some high-quality wheat bread, a thick slice of ripe tomato, and some crisp butter lettuce.

Serves 2–4

8 ounces skinless sunfish fillets
1 rib celery, finely minced
1 shallot, finely minced
2 tablespoons finely minced tarragon
2 tablespoons mayonnaise
your favorite bread

Put 2 cups of water into a medium saucepan and place over medium-high heat. Bring to a gentle simmer, reduce heat to low, and add fish fillets. Poach until just cooked through, about 2 to 4 minutes. Once the fish is cooked, quickly place the fillets in an ice bath and let chill. After the fish is cold, remove from the ice bath and flake apart. In a small mixing bowl, stir together the fish, celery, shallot, tarragon, and mayo. Season with salt and pepper and spread onto your favorite bread. Top as desired.

Crispy Roasted Sunfish with Braised Endive, Cauliflower Puree, and Orange Sauce

THIS DISH MIGHT SEEM A little more elaborate, but it's still incredibly easy. The crispy fish, melt-in-your-mouth endive, and creamy cauliflower puree all come together under the vibrant orange sauce, making for a restaurant-quality entrée that will have your friends thinking you're a master chef.

Serves 4

- 2 cups heavy cream
- ½ head cauliflower, chopped
- 4 tablespoons butter
- 2 tablespoons olive oil
- 4 Belgian endive, quartered
- ½ cup chicken stock
- ½ cup orange juice
- 1 teaspoon red chile flakes
- 4 large (or 8 small) sunfish fillets, skin scored

Place cream and chopped cauliflower in a medium saucepan and bring to a simmer. Cook until cauliflower is fork tender. Carefully transfer mixture to a blender, add 2 tablespoons butter, and puree until smooth. Season with salt and pepper to taste.

Add 1 tablespoon butter and 1 tablespoon olive oil to a skillet over medium-high heat. After the butter has melted, add in the endive and sear all sides to a golden brown. Add the chicken stock, orange juice, and chile flakes and cook until the liquid is fully reduced and the endive is fork tender.

Add 1 tablespoon butter and 1 tablespoon olive oil to a pan over medium-high heat. After the butter has melted, add in fish fillets skin side down and cook until skin is crispy, about 2 minutes. Flip the fish and cook for an additional 30 to 60 seconds.

Spread puree on serving plates and top with the endive and fish.

Oven-Roasted Sunfish, Fennel, and Orange with Potato Puree and Chile Citrus Beurre Blanc

THIS DISH IS DELICIOUS AND, despite the chile, not intensely spicy. The fennel and the orange lend a profound sweetness, while the potato puree gives some nice earthy tones. The beurre blanc is light and refreshing with just a touch of heat. Don't fear the amount of butter used in the sauce. While it may seem like a lot, very little fat is used in the rest of the dish.

Serves 2–4

2 cups milk
2 medium potatoes, chopped
2 small onions, 1 roughly chopped and 1 sliced
8 tablespoons (1 stick) butter
1 bulb fennel, thinly sliced, plus 1 tablespoon fronds, finely chopped
2 Cara Cara oranges, segmented, or substitute navel oranges, segmented
1 red finger (or Fresno) chile, finely chopped
2 tablespoons olive oil
12 small skinless sunfish fillets
1 tablespoon cider vinegar
2 tablespoons fresh orange juice

Preheat oven to 425 degrees. Add milk, potatoes, and roughly chopped onion to a medium saucepan and bring to a simmer. Season with a pinch of salt and cook until the potatoes are fork tender. Use a slotted spoon to remove potatoes and onions from the milk; transfer vegetables to a blender with 2 tablespoons butter. Blend to a smooth puree, adding milk as needed to reach desired consistency.

Toss together sliced fennel, sliced onion, orange segments, and half of the chile with olive oil. Place on a baking tray and roast for 15 to 20 minutes. Season with salt.

Grease a baking tray with nonstick spray. Season sunfish fillets with salt and pepper and place on the tray. Roast until fillets are cooked through, 2 to 3 minutes depending on size.

Stir together vinegar and orange juice in a small saucepan over medium-high heat and cook until the liquid is reduced to about 1 tablespoon. Remove from heat and add in the remaining 6 tablespoons butter, whisking constantly until butter is fully melted and sauce is thoroughly combined. Stir in the remaining chile and the fennel fronds.

Portion the potato puree onto serving plates, top with the fennel and orange mixture and the sunfish fillets, and drizzle on the butter sauce. Enjoy!

Hot Fried Sunnies with Pickled Onion and Chile Mayo

THIS GREAT TWIST ON THE classic north woods sunfish fry features just a little kick. The recipe is really flexible, and if you want it hotter, simply increase the amount of cayenne.

Serves 2–4

1 tablespoon sugar
¼ cup cider vinegar
½ cup finely chopped onion
½ cup mayonnaise
1 red chile, finely chopped
1 cup all-purpose flour
2 tablespoons cayenne
1 large egg
1 tablespoon hot sauce
1 pound skinless sunfish fillets
2 ½ cups vegetable oil
lemon and chopped green onion for garnish

Place the sugar and vinegar in a small saucepan and bring to a boil. Cook, stirring, until the sugar dissolves, remove from heat, and stir in the onions. Set aside to cool.

In a small mixing bowl, stir together mayo, cooled and drained onions, and chopped chiles. Season with salt to taste. Refrigerate until needed.

Set up a basic frying station. Stir together flour and cayenne, then divide the mixture equally onto two large plates. Crack the egg into a bowl, stir in the hot sauce, and beat until smooth. Dredge each fish fillet through the first plate of flour to coat, then dip in the egg mixture, allowing excess to drip away, and then re-dredge using the second plate of flour. Place fillets on a plate or a rack.

In a medium to large saucepan over medium-high heat, warm the oil to approximately 350 degrees. Add in 3 to 4 fillets at a time and fry until golden brown, about 2 to 3 minutes. Drain on a paper towel–lined plate. Season with salt.

Place fillets on a serving platter and garnish with lemon or green onion along with the pickled onion chile mayo. Dig in!

Sunfish Paella

PAELLA IS ONE OF THOSE quintessential Spanish dishes that is both comforting and incredibly flavorful. The soft rice is spiked with saffron and paprika, and the roasted red peppers give a pop of delicious sweetness. You can change up this recipe a few different ways. Leave the fish skin on and crisp it up first to give a nice texture to the dish. Or prepare the fish skin off, adding the fillets closer to the end. You can also throw in other seafood items like mussels, clams, or shrimp. And it's easy to adjust the heat level. If you like it spicy, add chiles or swap them out for a hotter variety. If you like it mild, just use the roasted red peppers or leave them out altogether. It is your paella, after all.

Serves 2–4

- 2–4 tablespoons olive oil
- 6–8 sunfish fillets (see head note)
- 3 ½ cups chicken stock
- 1 teaspoon saffron threads
- 1 tablespoon Spanish paprika
- 1 small to medium onion, chopped
- ½ fresh red bell pepper, chopped
- 1 green onion, chopped, plus more for garnish
- 1 tablespoon tomato paste
- 2 tablespoons sherry vinegar
- 1 cup Spanish Bomba (or Arborio) rice
- 1 cup frozen peas
- 1 cup roughly chopped cilantro
- 1 roasted red bell pepper, cut into strips

If preparing the fish skin on, add 2 tablespoons olive oil to a large skillet over medium-high heat. When the oil begins to shimmer and smoke, add in the fillets skin side down and cook until skin is crisp and golden brown. Do NOT flip. Remove from pan and set aside.

Stir together stock, saffron, and Spanish paprika in a medium saucepan over medium-high heat and bring to a simmer. Reduce heat and maintain a light simmer until the stock is needed.

To a large skillet over medium-high heat (if you pre-seared your fish, use the same pan), add 2 tablespoons olive oil, onion, and fresh red pepper. Cook until the onions become translucent, then add in the green onion and tomato paste. Cook until the tomato paste fully coats the rest of the vegetables and begins to caramelize. Add vinegar and cook, scraping up any browned bits, until the vinegar has almost fully reduced, then add in rice and cook for 2 to 3 minutes. Stir in the frozen peas and then pour in 2 cups of the stock, reduce heat to medium, and allow to simmer until the liquid has been fully absorbed. If the rice is not fully cooked, stir in an additional half cup stock. Repeat this process until the rice is fully cooked but still a little loose.

For pre-seared fillets, nestle them into the rice and cook through. For skinless fillets, nestle them into the rice and cover the skillet to allow the fish to cook from the bottom and steam through from the top. Garnish with cilantro, roasted red pepper strips, and additional green onion if desired.

TIP Roasted red peppers are available in a jar, but it's easy to roast a red pepper on a gas stovetop. Just place the pepper over the flame to char the skin, rotating until the entire outside of the pepper is blackened. Seal the pepper in a paper bag or covered bowl for 10 to 15 minutes to steam. Peel away the skin and cut open the pepper and discard the seeds.

Sunfish and Kimchi Fried Rice

NO LIE: KIMCHI FRIED RICE is one of my all-time favorite foods. Its mélange of huge flavors all marry beautifully together. It's also easy to make since the best way to do it usually involves leftover rice. Basically all you have to do is throw all your ingredients together in a hot wok and kiss them with some soy sauce and you're good to go. And like most things in life, it's best with a fried egg on top.

Chinese sausage, with flavors of soy and ginger throughout, is truly unique. It's also cured and dried, giving it a texture more akin to beef jerky than fresh sausage. If you can get it, you absolutely should, but if you can't, just use your favorite sausage or a teriyaki-flavored beef jerky.

Serves 2–4

vegetable oil
1 large egg per person
½ cup chopped Chinese sausage (see head note)
1 bunch green onions, white and green parts separated, chopped
1 cup roughly chopped kimchi
1 clove garlic, chopped
1 tablespoon freshly grated ginger
2 cups skinless sunfish fillets cut into half-inch pieces
3 cups cooked white rice
⅓ cup soy sauce
1 tablespoon sesame oil
1 tablespoon Sriracha
1 tablespoon rice wine vinegar
sesame seeds
lime wedges

Add 1 tablespoon vegetable oil to a small skillet over medium-low heat. Crack in eggs and cook until perfectly sunny-side up. Remove from skillet and set aside.

To a large pan (or wok), add 2 tablespoons vegetable oil. When oil is shimmering, add in Chinese sausage and cook until it starts to turn golden brown. Stir in the white part of the green onions, kimchi, garlic, ginger, and fish and cook for about 2 minutes, until the fish is almost cooked through. Add in the rice, soy sauce, sesame oil, Sriracha, and vinegar and stir to combine. Cook until rice is warmed through. Portion into bowls, top with egg, and garnish with green part of green onions, sesame seeds, and lime wedges.

TIP For the best fried rice, use cooked rice that has had a chance to dry out—like leftover rice from Chinese takeout or delivery.

Sunfish and Asparagus Risotto

FEW THINGS ARE BETTER THAN a warm bowl of homemade risotto, and this one makes use of the humble sunfish. This dish is truly timely, as sunfish season and asparagus season overlap nicely in the spring. The saffron brings a floral undertone to the dish while providing its signature rich yellow color. Make a double batch and use the leftovers for Sunfish Arancini (page 156).

Serves 2–4

4 cups fish or chicken stock
pinch saffron (4–6 threads)
1 pound skinless sunfish fillets
vegetable oil
butter
1 large shallot, finely minced
1 ⅓ cups Arborio rice
1 cup white wine
2 cups asparagus cut into one-inch pieces
½ cup grated Parmesan cheese
1 tablespoon red chile flakes

Add the stock and saffron to a medium saucepan over medium-high heat. Bring to a simmer, reduce heat to low, and gently place in fish fillets. Poach until fish is just cooked through and flaky, about 3 to 4 minutes. Remove from the liquid and flake apart into chunks. Set the fish aside; keep the stock warm over medium-low heat.

Add 2 tablespoons vegetable oil and 2 tablespoons butter to a large skillet over medium heat. After the butter has melted, add shallots and cook until they start to become translucent. Add rice and gently toast for about 2 to 3 minutes, stirring to coat with the oil and butter. Stir in the white wine and cook until most has been absorbed by the rice, then stir in the asparagus. Add in 2 cups of the warm stock and stir until the rice absorbs the majority of the stock. Repeat until stock is gone and rice is cooked all the way through. Add in the flaked fish, Parmesan, chile flakes, and 2 tablespoons butter, folding to combine. Season with salt and pepper to taste and serve.

Sunfish Arancini with Lemon Aioli

THIS DISH IS THE PERFECT use for any leftover risotto you might have—so much so that I always try to have leftovers so I can make it. The next day, after the risotto has sat overnight in the fridge, roll it into balls and deep-fry to make one of the best snacks ever. The lemony aioli makes Sunfish and Asparagus Risotto (page 154) all the better!

Serves 2–4

¼ cup mayonnaise
2 tablespoons fresh lemon juice
1 clove garlic, grated
2 cups leftover risotto
1 cup all-purpose flour
1 large egg, beaten
1 cup panko bread crumbs
vegetable oil

Stir together the mayo, lemon juice, and garlic in a small bowl. Season with salt and pepper and refrigerate until needed.

Using your hands, take about a golf ball–sized amount of risotto and roll into a ball. Repeat until the risotto is gone, making about 8 balls, or arancini.

Set up a basic frying station by adding the flour to a small plate, the egg to a small bowl, and the panko to another small plate. Dredge the risotto balls in the flour to coat, dip in the egg mixture, and then cover with panko. Refrigerate for at least 20 minutes.

To a medium saucepan over medium-high heat, add enough vegetable oil to just cover the arancini, but do not fill the pan more than halfway. Heat to 350 degrees and then add balls 2 to 3 at a time and fry until golden brown, about 3 to 5 minutes. Remove from oil and drain on a paper towel–lined plate. Season with salt as soon as they come out of the fryer. Serve with a small side of the aioli.

Sunfish and Shells with Dill Cream

THIS DISH IS EASY TO throw together on any night of the week. Its big, bold flavors shine especially bright during the summer months.

Serves 2–4

4 cups dry shell-shaped pasta
butter
2 tablespoons minced red onion
1 clove garlic, minced
2 tablespoons fresh lemon juice and 2 tablespoons freshly grated lemon zest
2 cups heavy cream
¼ cup freshly grated Parmesan cheese
8 ounces skinless sunfish fillets, cut into half-inch pieces
¼ cup roughly chopped dill, plus more for garnish

Place a pot of water over medium-high heat and add a pinch of salt. Bring to a boil and add pasta. Cook about 1 minute less than the package instructions; pasta should be just a bit above al dente, tender but still firm. Drain and set aside.

Melt 2 tablespoons butter in a skillet over medium-high heat. Stir in onions and cook until they start to become translucent. Stir in garlic and cook for 1 minute, then add lemon juice. Once the lemon juice is mostly reduced, stir in the cream, bring to a simmer, and cook until it starts to reduce and thicken. Whisk in Parmesan cheese until fully melted. Reduce heat to low, add the fish, and let it gently poach in the sauce, about 2 minutes. Stir in the lemon zest and dill and simmer for another minute. Add the pasta to the sauce and stir to combine. Remove from heat and let sit for about 2 minutes. Serve with a few additional dill fronds for garnish.

Sunfish Hash

NO JOKE: THIS IS THE ultimate fisherman's breakfast. Bust this one out for your friends on a camping trip and you'll be a hero, guaranteed. Or just make it at home for a simple Sunday breakfast. The mix of potatoes, peppers, pancetta, and fish are a perfect, high-protein way to start your day. Pro tip: be sure to throw a fried egg on top.

Serves 2–4

1 pound potatoes, cut into half-inch cubes
vegetable oil
butter
½ cup cubed pancetta (or bacon)
½ red onion, roughly chopped
8 ounces skinless sunfish fillets, cut into half-inch pieces
1 roasted red bell pepper, roughly chopped
2 tablespoons roughly chopped tarragon

Place potatoes in a pot of cold water and set over medium-high heat. Cook until the water is boiling and the potatoes are nearly fork tender. Drain potatoes and set aside.

Add 2 tablespoons vegetable oil and 2 tablespoons butter to a skillet over medium-high heat. After the butter has melted, stir in the potatoes and pancetta and cook until potatoes start to turn golden brown. Stir in the onions and cook until soft and translucent. Stir in fish and roasted red pepper and cook until the fish is just cooked through, about 2 to 3 minutes. Stir in the tarragon and serve.

Trout-Stuffed Mushrooms with Baked Eggs (page 180)

TROUT

Trout Tartine

ONE OF THE THINGS I love about good tartines (aside from the fact that they're absolutely delicious) is that they sound WAY fancier than they really are. *Tartine* is simply a French name for an open-faced sandwich, but it works so well with trout that your friends and family won't be the wiser when they sit down to eat their fancy sandwiches. This recipe is great for leftover trout, but you can also cook some up expressly for this purpose: just let it cool before you make your tartines.

Serves 2–4

4 slices pumpernickel bread
½ cup chive (or herbed) cream cheese
2 cups cooked, flaked trout
½ cup thinly sliced red onion
chives
olive oil (optional)

Toast the bread to desired level of doneness—ideally, crisp on the outside and still chewy on the inside. Spread approximately 2 tablespoons of cream cheese on each slice and then top evenly with trout, red onion, and fresh chives. Cut in half, lightly drizzle with olive oil if desired, and serve.

Rainbow Trout Niçoise

TRADITIONALLY YOU'LL SEE THIS DINNER salad done with tuna and every once in a while with salmon, but trout works equally well and—bonus—is a much more sustainable species. This combination packs a big flavor punch: the salty, briny olives help to pull out some of the sweet flavors in the fish, and the contrast in textures from the potatoes and the crispy green beans is near perfection.

Serves 2–4

- 2 tablespoons mustard
- 2 tablespoons champagne vinegar
- olive oil
- 1 cup pitted, sliced Kalamata olives
- 1 cup halved cherry tomatoes
- 1 cup halved or quartered boiled new potatoes
- 1 cup roughly chopped green beans
- 4 (4- to 6-ounce) skin-on trout fillets
- 4 large hard-boiled eggs, sliced

Add mustard, vinegar, and approximately 6 tablespoons of olive oil to a small bowl, whisking to combine. Season with salt.

In a medium mixing bowl, toss together olives, tomatoes, potatoes, and green beans. Dress lightly with approximately 2 tablespoons of the vinaigrette and season with salt and pepper.

Pat fish fillets dry and season with salt. Add 2 tablespoons olive oil to a skillet over medium-high heat and then the fillets, skin side down. Cook until the skin is crispy and golden brown, about 2 to 3 minutes. Flip and finish cooking for an additional 1 to 2 minutes. Place the fish on a serving platter and top with the salad. Garnish with egg slices and drizzle with additional vinaigrette as desired.

Smoked Trout Kale Niçoise

ANOTHER TAKE ON THE CLASSIC tuna Niçoise, this one features chilled, flaked smoked trout instead of freshly seared fillets. Using kale as the primary green helps bump up the nutrition factor while keeping things local. If you can't find smoked trout, smoked Alaskan salmon will work, or choose traditional and sustainable yellowfin tuna from Hawaii.

Serves 2–4

2 tablespoons red wine vinegar
1 tablespoon Dijon mustard
¼ cup olive oil
2 cups shredded kale
2 cups deboned, chunked smoked trout
2 large hardboiled eggs, sliced
1 cup chopped boiled potatoes
1 cup halved or quartered cherry tomatoes
¼ cup toasted sunflower seeds
½ cup pitted and chopped Kalamata olives

In a mixing bowl, combine vinegar, mustard, and olive oil, whisking until thoroughly combined. Season with salt and pepper to taste.

Divide kale among serving plates and top with equal portions of all the other ingredients. Drizzle with dressing and serve.

Smoked Trout and Pickled Yellow Beet Salad with Crème Fraîche

THIS MIGHT JUST BE MY favorite salad. The smoked trout and pickled beets play well off of each other, making each forkful an absolute delight. For this salad, I do two different preparations of quick pickles: one for the beets and one for the pearl onions. The pickling takes very little time, and the technique lends itself to a wide variety of vegetables and vinegars. Garnish with a few microgreens or fresh herbs if you have them on hand, or a few thin slices of raw yellow beet.

Serves 2–4

1 cup champagne vinegar
6 tablespoons sugar
1 cup medium yellow beets, peeled and cut into half-inch chunks
1 sprig fresh dill
½ cup red wine vinegar
1 tablespoon peppercorns
1 cup purple pearl onions, peeled and halved
8 ounces smoked trout, flaked
olive oil
crème fraîche
1 radish, thinly sliced

Place champagne vinegar in a saucepan over medium-high heat and add 4 tablespoons sugar. Simmer until sugar dissolves, then add in beets and dill. Reduce to medium heat and simmer until beets become fork tender. Remove from heat and cool to room temperature before placing beets and liquid in the refrigerator.

Place red wine vinegar, remaining 2 tablespoons sugar, peppercorns, and a pinch of salt in a saucepan over medium heat and simmer until the sugar dissolves. Add the onions and simmer for no longer than 30 seconds. Remove from heat and cool to room temperature before placing onions and liquid in the refrigerator.

Once the beets are chilled, add them to a mixing bowl with the smoked trout. Add in 1 tablespoon beet pickling liquid (see tip) and about 1 tablespoon olive oil. Toss to combine.

On serving plates, add about a tablespoon of crème fraîche and smooth it with a spoon to create a thin, circular layer. Divide the trout and beet mixture evenly among the serving plates and garnish with pickled onions and radish slices.

TIP Use excess pickling liquid to pickle more vegetables—simply drop them in—or to make dressings for other salads.

Trout, Corn, and Black Bean Salad

THIS RIFF ON A FAVORITE summer salad is always a big hit at a backyard cookout. The fresh flavors make it a perfect side dish during the hotter days of the year. Set it alongside a nicely grilled flank steak, and you've got yourself a different kind of surf and turf.

Serves 4+

2 cups cooked, flaked trout
1 (15-ounce) can sweet corn, drained
1 (15-ounce) can black beans, rinsed and drained
1 cup chopped tomato
½ cup chopped red onion
½ cup chopped cilantro
1 serrano chile, finely minced
2 tablespoons olive oil
juice of ½ lime

Add all ingredients to a large mixing bowl and toss to combine. Season with salt and pepper.

Trout with Cucumber Salad

TROUT PAIRS WELL WITH BRIGHT Scandinavian flavors, and one of my favorite Scandinavian sides happens to be this delicious and simple cucumber salad. While the salad could be eaten right away, it benefits from a marinating time of at least an hour. For a full and vibrant meal, serve with roasted or mashed cauliflower or potatoes.

Serves 2–4

1 cucumber, thinly sliced
½ red onion, thinly sliced
½ cup seasoned rice wine vinegar
4 (6- to 8-ounce) skinless trout fillets
2 tablespoons olive oil

Place the cucumber and red onion in a large mixing bowl, drizzle with vinegar, and season with salt and pepper. Toss to combine. Marinate in the refrigerator for at least 1 hour before serving (see head note).

Preheat oven to 425 degrees. Line a baking tray with aluminum foil. Pat the trout fillets dry, place on baking tray, drizzle with olive oil, and season with salt and pepper. Bake for 8 to 10 minutes or until the trout is just cooked through and flaky. Top the trout with the cucumber salad and serve.

Pan-Roasted Rainbow Trout with Oven-Roasted Mushrooms, Celeriac Puree, and Red Wine Sauce

THIS FAIRLY SIMPLE ENTRÉE HAS huge flavor. Rainbow trout is available year round, but this dish is best in the spring or fall. If you can't find fresh rainbow trout, wild-caught Alaskan salmon or farm-raised arctic char would be great, sustainable substitutes.

Serves 4

butter
1 celeriac, peeled and cubed
½ cup heavy cream
1 cup red wine
1 sprig fresh thyme
1 cup red wine vinegar
¼ cup dried cherries or cranberries
2 cups chopped mushrooms (see tip)
olive oil
2 fillets skin-on rainbow trout, trimmed and halved

Preheat oven to 425 degrees. Melt 1 tablespoon butter in a medium saucepan over medium-high heat and add celeriac. Cook, stirring, until the celeriac turns translucent and softens. Stir in heavy cream and simmer until celeriac is fork tender. Mash celeriac or use a blender to puree to desired texture. Let sit over very low heat until needed.

Warm red wine with thyme in a small saucepan over medium-high heat, cooking to reduce liquid by half. Stir in vinegar and dried fruit and reduce until sauce is the consistency of syrup; strain sauce and discard fruit.

Add mushrooms to a roasting pan, drizzle with 1 tablespoon olive oil, and season with a pinch of salt and a few cracks of freshly ground pepper. Roast until mushrooms become golden brown, about 5 minutes.

Pat trout fillets dry and season on both sides with salt and pepper. Melt 2 tablespoons butter in a skillet over medium heat. Place fillets skin side down and cook until skin is golden brown, about 3 to 4 minutes. Flip fillets and cook through, about 1 to 2 minutes. Serve trout on top of the celeriac puree, garnish with mushrooms, and drizzle with sauce.

TIP A good mix of wild mushrooms is best. Be sure to wipe clean before chopping.

Steamed Trout with Ginger and Green Onions

AN EXTREMELY HEALTHY DISH PACKED full of flavor, this one is great for summertime when you want something fresh, light, and satisfying. Pair it with white or brown rice for the perfect meal.

Serves 2–4

vegetable oil
2 cloves garlic, thinly sliced
¼ cup fresh ginger cut into thin matchsticks
green onions, ½ cup white parts, finely chopped, and ½ cup green parts, cut into one-inch pieces
2 tablespoons soy sauce
2 tablespoons mirin
1 tablespoon sesame oil
1 tablespoon rice wine vinegar
2 (8- to 10-ounce) skin-on trout fillets
1 Fresno chile, finely minced
hot cooked rice

Add 3 tablespoons vegetable oil and garlic to a large skillet over medium-low heat and cook gently to infuse the oil with garlic flavor, about 3 to 4 minutes. Add ginger and green onion white parts and cook, stirring, for about 2 to 3 minutes. Stir in soy sauce, mirin, sesame oil, and vinegar. Push the ingredients to the sides of the skillet and add fish fillets skin side down and ¼ cup water. Cover and steam for 5 to 6 minutes or until the fish is just cooked through and flakes apart easily. Gently peel the fish away from the skin, garnish with green onion greens and Fresno chile, and serve with vegetable mixture and a side of rice.

Red Wine Poached Trout

THIS FUN AND SIMPLE WAY of preparing trout not only imparts a nice hit of acidity and flavor to the fish but also gives the exterior a really cool purple hue while leaving the inside flesh a beautiful soft pink. It takes only minutes, but the result is really impressive and would work well at a dinner party served along with a side of creamy mashed or roasted potatoes and some roasted greens.

Serves 2–4

1 cup red wine
1 cup red wine vinegar
1 shallot, roughly chopped
4 sprigs fresh thyme
1 teaspoon peppercorns
4 (4- to 6-ounce) skinless trout fillets
4 tablespoons cold, unsalted butter, cut into one-inch chunks

Stir together red wine, vinegar, shallot, thyme, and peppercorns in a small saucepan. Bring to a boil and then reduce heat to medium low to maintain a gentle simmer. Place the fish fillets in the wine mixture and gently poach for 4 to 5 minutes or until the fish is just cooked through. Remove fish and set aside. Pour the wine mixture through a sieve into a bowl, discard the solids, and add the liquid back to the pot. Place over medium-high heat, bring mixture to a boil, and cook until reduced to about ½ cup. Remove from heat and cool slightly. Slowly whisk in the butter one piece at a time until fully incorporated. Drizzle the fish with the wine sauce and serve.

Trout Amandine

SOMETIMES THE CLASSICS ARE CLASSICS for a reason, and this one lives up to its rich history. It's not uncommon to see amandine done with salmon, which makes trout the perfect substitute. The flavorful green beans and almonds give amazing salty, sweet, spicy, and earthy flavors to the dish, and their textures are a perfect complement to the simply roasted fish, served with a side of baked or boiled potatoes.

Serves 2–4

1 pound trout fillet(s)
olive oil
2 cups trimmed green beans
1 cup almonds
1 tablespoon sesame oil
1 tablespoon rice wine vinegar
2 tablespoons soy sauce
1 teaspoon freshly grated ginger
1 clove garlic, finely minced
1 teaspoon red chile flakes
¼ cup thinly sliced red onion (optional)

Preheat oven to 450 degrees. Pat the fish dry, place on a roasting pan, drizzle with 2 tablespoons olive oil, and season with salt and pepper. Roast for about 5 minutes or until the fish is just cooked through.

Add 2 tablespoons olive oil to a skillet over high heat. When the oil is shimmering, add in the green beans and cook evenly in the hot oil, allowing all sides to brown, about 2 minutes. Stir in the almonds, sesame oil, vinegar, soy sauce, ginger, garlic, and chile flakes. Toss to combine, and cook for an additional 1 to 2 minutes or until sauce turns into a glaze and beans and almonds are evenly coated. Place the fish on a serving platter with beans and almonds and garnish with sliced onions.

Trout Quiche with Bacon and Leeks

I'M NOT SURE I'VE EVER had a bad dish that featured bacon and leeks, but the addition of trout really elevates this quiche into a special brunch dish. Top with a dollop of sour cream and fresh chives if you like. No matter how you eat it, you're going to love it.

Serves 4–8

6 strips bacon, cut into quarter-inch matchsticks
2 (4- to 6-ounce) skinless trout fillets
2 leeks, rinsed well and roughly chopped
dough for single-crust pie
5 large eggs
¼ cup heavy cream

Preheat oven to 350 degrees. Place a skillet over medium-high heat and add sliced bacon. Cook until bacon is crisp and fat has rendered. Use a slotted spoon to remove bacon, leaving fat in the pan. Place the fish fillets into the hot skillet and sear for about 2 minutes on each side or until just cooked through. Remove from pan and set aside. Add leeks to the pan and cook, stirring, until leeks soften and begin to become translucent. Return the bacon to the pan, season with salt, and stir to combine.

Prepare pie crust according to package instructions or recipe directions; line a pie plate with dough. Pour bacon and leek mixture into crust. Flake trout and place pieces on top of mixture. In a medium mixing bowl, whisk together eggs and cream to thoroughly combine. Season with salt and pepper and pour into pie crust. Bake until eggs have fully set and top just starts to brown, about 30 to 40 minutes. Cool quiche to room temperate before serving.

Trout-Stuffed Mushrooms with Baked Eggs

THIS DISH WAS THE RESULT of an interesting experiment, and I'm happy to say that it worked out beautifully. The mushroom caps are the perfect vessel for the fish, asparagus, and onions, and maple syrup adds sweetness to highlight the earthy elements of the mushrooms and asparagus. Or skip the syrup for a lovely appetizer or light dinner, served with a side of dressed greens.

Serves 2–4

2 cups cooked, flaked trout
1 cup roughly chopped asparagus
¼ cup roughly chopped red onion
2 tablespoons maple syrup
4 large portabella mushroom caps, cleaned
4 large eggs
chives

Preheat oven to 450 degrees. In a mixing bowl, toss together fish, asparagus, onion, and syrup. Season with salt.

Remove and discard the stems and gills from the mushroom caps and divide trout mixture evenly among the caps. Place on a baking tray and crack one egg on top of each mushroom. Bake until eggs are just set but yolks are still runny, about 5 to 7 minutes. Garnish with fresh chives and serve.

Spanish Trout Tortilla with Roasted Red Peppers

NOT DISSIMILAR TO AN OMELET, a frittata, or even a quiche, this egg and potato dish also happens to pair very well with trout. The addition of sweet roasted red peppers and a touch of sherry helps ramp up the delicious Spanish flavors, making a dish perfect for breakfast, lunch, or dinner.

Serves 4–8

6 large eggs
2 tablespoons sherry
vegetable oil
butter
1 cup boiled potatoes cut into quarter-inch pieces
1 cup roasted red bell pepper cut into quarter-inch pieces
½ cup roughly chopped red onion
2 cups cooked, flaked trout

Preheat oven to 400 degrees. In a mixing bowl, whisk together eggs and sherry. Season with salt and pepper.

Add 2 tablespoons oil and 2 tablespoons butter to a large skillet over medium-high heat. When the butter is melted and frothy, add in potatoes, red peppers, onions, and fish. Cook, stirring, for about 1 minute, then pour in the egg mixture. Stir to combine, and as the egg starts to form large curds, place skillet in the oven and cook for approximately 20 minutes or until egg has set and starts to brown around the edges.

Remove skillet from oven and cover with a large plate or platter. Flip over the skillet to release the egg mixture onto the plate. Add the egg mixture back to the skillet, now with the bottom side up, place back in the oven, and bake for another 10 minutes or until the egg is fully set into one large egg "pancake." Remove from the oven and turn out onto a platter. Cut into wedges and serve.

Walleye Cakes (page 196)

WALLEYE

Walleye Lettuce Wraps

YOU MAY HAVE ENCOUNTERED A variation of these lettuce wraps at one of those swanky, "high-end" Asian restaurant chains, but I promise this flavorful appetizer (or light meal) is so easy to make that you'll never want to order out for them again. Well, maybe *never* is too strong a word. Still, they are delicious and take only a few minutes to make: you'll be able to eat them all the time—and since they're also healthy and light, you won't have to worry about doing so, either.

Serves 2–4

vegetable oil
4 (4- to 6-ounce) skinless walleye fillets
1 cup gently crushed cashews
4 green onions, roughly chopped
1 clove garlic, finely minced
1 tablespoon freshly grated ginger
1 serrano (or Fresno) chile, finely minced
1 teaspoon sesame oil
1 tablespoon rice wine vinegar
2 tablespoons soy sauce, plus more for serving
2 tablespoons hoisin sauce
½–1 tablespoon Sriracha
1 tablespoon mirin
2 tablespoons roughly chopped cilantro
2 tablespoons roughly chopped basil
1 tablespoon fresh lime juice
1 head iceberg lettuce

Add 2 tablespoons vegetable oil to a skillet over medium-high heat. Once the oil is shimmering, add in the fish fillets and cook for about 2 minutes on each side. Break up the fish into small pieces using a fork or spatula. Stir in the cashews, onions, garlic, ginger, and chile and continue to cook until the onions start to soften, about 2 minutes. Stir in the sesame oil, vinegar, soy sauce, hoisin, Sriracha, and mirin and continue cooking until the sauce reduces and thickens. Stir in the fresh herbs and lime juice.

Remove the core from the head of lettuce and separate the leaves into individual cups or wrappers. Serve the mixture inside the lettuce wrappers along with a side of soy sauce.

Walleye Waldorf

SOMETIMES OLD SCHOOL IS A great way to go. Classics are usually classics for a reason, right? This salad predates retro and goes all the way back to the 1890s, originating from the Waldorf Hotel in New York City, but its freshness and brightness encompass a modern approach to flavor building, utilizing savory, sweet, salty, and earthy elements, all of which work quite nicely with walleye.

Serves 2–4

2 (4- to 6-ounce) skinless walleye fillets, cut into one-inch pieces
1 sweet red apple, cut into quarter-inch cubes (about 1 cup)
1 rib celery, cut into quarter-inch pieces (about 1 cup)
1 cup crushed walnuts
2 tablespoons roughly chopped fresh tarragon
1 cup mayonnaise
juice of ½ lemon
1 tablespoon champagne vinegar
iceberg lettuce

Put 3 cups water in a medium saucepan and place over medium-high heat. Bring to a simmer, reduce heat to low, add in the walleye pieces, and poach until just cooked through, about 4 minutes. Quickly place the fish pieces in an ice bath and let chill. After the fish is fully chilled, remove from ice bath and flake with your hands. Place the fish in a mixing bowl along with all of the other ingredients (except lettuce) and gently stir to combine. Season with salt and serve on a bed of fresh iceberg lettuce.

Grilled Walleye with Grilled Apricot and Herb Salad

LOOKING FOR THE PERFECT SUMMERTIME fish dish? This one is a good go-to. It makes use of ripe stone fruit along with fresh herbs, onions, and a bit of chile for some heat. It's a great one for the grill, or if you've got an indoor griddle pan, that'll work too.

Serves 2–4

4 ripe apricots, pitted and cut into wedges
olive oil
¼ red onion, thinly sliced
1 Fresno chile, finely minced
2 tablespoons thinly sliced basil
2 tablespoons roughly chopped fresh tarragon
1 tablespoon sherry vinegar
4 (4- to 6-ounce) skinless walleye fillets

Place the apricot wedges in a small mixing bowl, toss with 2 tablespoons olive oil, and season with salt. Place a griddle pan over medium-high heat. Once it's hot, add the apricots to the pan and sear just long enough to get hard grill marks on both sides; place apricots back in the mixing bowl. Stir in the onion, chile, basil, tarragon, and vinegar. Season with salt. Set aside.

Drizzle the walleye fillets with 2 tablespoons olive oil and season with salt. Place the fillets on the hot griddle pan and cook for about 2 minutes on each side or until cooked through and flaky. Portion the salad onto serving plates, top with the walleye, and go to town!

Classic Minnesota-Style Walleye Sandwich

ONE OF MY FAVORITE THINGS in this world is a big, fat walleye sandwich. Here in Minnesota, it's basically a staple and can be found in restaurants all across the state, but it's even better when you can make it for yourself at home. The sandwich itself is simply fried fish, some crisp lettuce, ripe tomatoes, and a tangy tartar sauce on a nice, soft bun. Feel free to use your favorite tartar sauce, but I've also included a recipe for one I like to whip together just for this sandwich.

Serves 4

¼ cup mayonnaise
¼ cup finely minced spicy bread and butter pickles
1 tablespoon pickle juice
1 ½ cups all-purpose flour
1 large egg, beaten
4 (4- to 6-ounce) skinless walleye fillets
vegetable oil
4 soft hoagie buns, split
lettuce
tomato

In a small mixing bowl, stir together mayo, pickles, and pickle juice. Season with salt to taste.

Set up a basic frying station. Divide the flour evenly between two large plates and place the beaten egg on a third. Dredge the fish fillets through the flour, then the egg, and then the second plate of flour, making sure they're completely coated. Set aside.

Place a medium to large skillet over medium-high heat and add about 1 to 2 cups oil, enough to come at least halfway up the fillets; do not fill the skillet more than halfway. Heat oil to 350 degrees, then add in 2 fillets and fry until the bottom side is completely golden brown and crisp, about 2 to 3 minutes. Flip and finish cooking the other side, another 2 to 3 minutes. Drain on a paper towel–lined plate, seasoning with salt as soon as the fish comes out of the fryer. Repeat with the other fillets. Place the fish on the slit hoagie bun, spread with tartar sauce, and pile on the lettuce and tomato.

Grilled Walleye Tacos with Mango Salsa

OF THE MILLIONS OF WAYS to put together a taco, this one might be the easiest. That there are so few ingredients is really the selling point, as it helps to emphasize the freshness of the fish. The walleye is perfect as its own entity, and the earthiness of the corn tortillas helps the natural sweetness of the fish to shine. Couple that with a sweet, savory, and spicy mango salsa and you may have created the perfect food.

Serves 2–4

1 cup finely chopped mango
½ cup finely chopped tomato
½ cup finely chopped red onion
juice of ½ lime
2 tablespoons finely chopped cilantro
4 (4- to 6-ounce) skinless walleye fillets
8 corn tortillas

Stir together the mango, tomato, onion, lime juice, and cilantro in a bowl. Season with salt and refrigerate until needed.

Pat the walleye fillets dry and season with salt. Place a grill pan over high heat and coat with nonstick spray. Add the fillets and cook for about 2 to 3 minutes on each side, then remove from heat. Cook the corn tortillas for about 10 seconds on each side. Flake the fish and place in tortillas. Top with the mango salsa.

Walleye Cakes

ANOTHER CLASSIC MINNESOTA CONCOCTION THAT'S just too good not to make, and it couldn't be more straightforward. It's 90 percent walleye and 10 percent other stuff, which means big, fresh walleye flavor. Spiked with a little onion, a little chile, some fresh herbs, and a little lemon mayo, these fish cakes work great as an appetizer or even a main course, served alongside some nice roasted veggies or potatoes.

Serves 2–4

½ cup mayonnaise
juice of ½ lemon
4 (4- to 6-ounce) skinless walleye fillets, cut into one-inch chunks
½ red onion, finely minced
1–2 Fresno chiles, finely minced
1 large egg yolk
2 tablespoons roughly chopped fresh tarragon
1 ½ cups panko bread crumbs
1 cup vegetable oil

Stir together mayo and lemon juice. Season with salt and pepper and refrigerate until needed.

Place walleye, onion, chiles, egg yolk, and tarragon in a blender and pulse to combine. The mixture shouldn't be perfectly smooth, but should come together easily. Form into about 8 (2-inch) patties. Refrigerate walleye cakes for at least 20 minutes. Dredge chilled cakes in panko and refrigerate for at least another 15 minutes.

Add vegetable oil to a skillet over medium-high heat. When oil is shimmering, add 4 fish cakes and cook until golden brown, about 2 to 3 minutes. Flip and cook for an additional 2 to 3 minutes. Drain cakes on a paper towel–lined plate. Repeat until all of the cakes have been cooked. Serve with a little lemon mayo and you're golden!

Walleye with Morels and Brown Butter

TASTING THIS DISH IS LIKE taking a bite out of Minnesota. The rich, earthy flavors of the morels and nutty brown butter play perfectly with the sweet, flaky, white flesh of the walleye, and a simple side of broccolini contributes just the right bit of freshness. Morels are a seasonal ingredient, making this a very special occasion dish, but you could also use dried morels: just reconstitute them first (see technique on page <?>). If you happen to have ramps (wild leeks), add them in with the morels for a little added punch.

Serves 4

4 (4- to 6-ounce) skinless walleye fillets
1 bunch broccolini
1 tablespoon olive oil
1 teaspoon red chile flakes
1 ½ tablespoons freshly grated lemon zest
6 tablespoons butter
4 ounces fresh morels

Preheat oven to broil. Season the walleye fillets with salt and place on a greased baking tray. Place broccolini on a greased baking tray, drizzle with olive oil, and sprinkle with chile flakes and 1 tablespoon lemon zest; season with salt. Place both the walleye and the broccolini in the oven and broil for about 5 minutes, until the walleye is just cooked through and the broccolini florets begin to char.

Melt butter in a medium skillet over medium-high heat and continue to cook, swirling pan, until it starts to turn a nutty brown color. Add in the morels and cook until they start to soften, then add in remaining ½ tablespoon lemon zest and season with salt.

Portion the broccolini onto serving plates, top with walleye and then morels, and drizzle with brown butter. Enjoy!

Walleye Basil Stir-Fry

THIS DISH HAS A LOT of flexibility: follow my suggestions of broccoli, carrots, pea pods, and some thinly sliced red onion, or feel free to experiment with whatever veggies you're into. When it all comes together with the basil, ginger, garlic, and stir-fry sauce, you're going to have yourself a winning dish. Note that the flaky nature of the walleye means the fish will break into smaller pieces during the cooking process.

Serves 2–4

- vegetable oil
- 2 cups mixed stir-fry vegetables (broccoli florets, snow pea pods, carrots, onions), cut or sliced into 1-inch pieces
- 2 (4- to 6-ounce) skinless walleye fillets, cut into one-inch pieces
- 1 clove garlic, finely minced
- 1 tablespoon freshly grated ginger
- 1 Fresno chile, finely minced
- 1 tablespoon mirin
- 2 tablespoons soy sauce
- 1 tablespoon hoisin or oyster sauce
- 1 teaspoon sesame oil
- ½ cup basil leaves (preferably Thai basil)
- hot cooked rice

Place a large skillet or wok over high heat and add 2 tablespoons vegetable oil. Heat oil to smoking, then toss in vegetable mix and cook, stirring, until softened and caramelized, about 2 to 3 minutes. Add in the fish, garlic, ginger, and chile and continue to cook, stirring, until the fish is just cooked through, about 2 to 3 minutes. Stir in the mirin, soy sauce, hoisin, sesame oil, and basil, and cook until the sauce starts to reduce and become sticky. Serve with a side of hot rice.

Grilled Walleye Succotash

IN TRUTH, THIS DISH LIES somewhere between a succotash and a southern-style hoppin' John, with grilled walleye in place of pork. Whatever you call it, the result is nothing shy of awesome and jammed full of flavor. It would make a simple side dish for a unique surf and turf, or serve it as is with some rice.

Serves 2–4

2 (4- to 6-ounce) skinless walleye fillets
vegetable oil
½ red bell pepper, roughly chopped
½ green or orange bell pepper, roughly chopped
½ large yellow onion, roughly chopped
1 cup frozen, fresh, or canned sweet corn
1 (15-ounce) can black-eyed peas, rinsed and drained
2 tablespoons roughly chopped fresh tarragon

Pat the walleye fillets dry and season with salt. Place a griddle pan over high heat and coat with nonstick spray. Add the fillets and cook for about 2 to 3 minutes on each side, then remove from heat.

Add 2 tablespoons vegetable oil to a skillet over medium-high heat. When the oil is shimmering, add in the peppers, onions, and corn. Cook, stirring, until onions soften and peppers brighten in color, about 5 to 6 minutes. Add in the black-eyed peas and continue to cook, stirring, until the beans are warmed through, about 3 to 4 minutes. Stir in the tarragon and break apart the walleye into the mixture. Cook, stirring, for an additional 1 to 2 minutes or until everything is well combined. Season with salt and serve.

Pasta al Luccio

HERE'S A RIFF ON AN old classic: pasta al tonno, traditionally made with canned tuna. Instead, I use walleye (or walleye pike), and by my best research, *luccio* is Italian for "pike." In either version, the fish cooks along with the sauce and eventually breaks down into small bits, creating a sort of briny ragu. The dish comes together easily, mostly in one pot (with the exception of the pasta), and is a great family meal for any day of the week.

Serves 2–4

2 tablespoons olive oil
½ cup finely chopped onion
1 clove garlic, finely minced
2 tablespoons capers
1 tablespoon dried oregano (or Italian herb mix)
1 teaspoon red chile flakes
2 (4- to 6-ounce) skinless walleye fillets, cut into one-inch pieces
1 cup white wine
1 (15-ounce) can crushed tomatoes
8 ounces dry angel hair pasta

Add olive oil to a large skillet over medium-high heat. Once the oil is shimmering, add in the onion and cook until it starts to soften and become translucent, then stir in the garlic, capers, oregano, and chile flakes and cook for an additional 2 minutes. Add in the fish and cook for an additional 2 minutes, breaking up the fish into small pieces. Stir in the wine and cook until reduced by about half, about 5 minutes. Stir in the crushed tomatoes and season with salt. Simmer for about 15 minutes.

Place a pot of water over high heat and add a big pinch of salt. Bring to a boil and add pasta. Cook about 1 to 2 minutes less than the package instructions; pasta should be just short of al dente, tender but still firm. Drain and add pasta immediately to the sauce to finish cooking. Garnish dish with fresh herbs of your choosing.

Midwestern Fisherman's Stew (page 213)

WHITEFISH

Tomato Tartare with Dill and Parsley Vinaigrette, Smoked Whitefish, and Avocado

THIS TARTARE IS LIKE A summertime dream come true while remaining completely loyal to its beefy origins. The dill and parsley vinaigrette enhances both the sweet and savory nature of the tomato, while the smoked whitefish brings everything to life. For an optimal plate-to-mouth delivery system, serve with buttery, crispy crostini.

Serves 2–4

2 cups peeled heirloom tomatoes (see tip), cut into quarter-inch cubes
2 tablespoons finely chopped shallot
1 avocado, cut into half-inch cubes
1 tablespoon fresh lemon juice
2 tablespoons chopped dill, plus more for garnish
2 tablespoons chopped parsley, plus more for garnish
2 tablespoons Dijon mustard
2 tablespoons champagne vinegar
1 tablespoon freshly grated lemon zest
6 tablespoons extra-virgin olive oil
1 cup flaked smoked whitefish

Place tomatoes in a colander with a pinch of salt and allow them to drain away some of their moisture. Add in the shallot and gently stir to combine.

Place the cubes of avocado in a small bowl, toss with the lemon juice and a pinch of salt, and set aside.

Add dill, parsley, mustard, vinegar, and lemon zest to a mixing bowl and whisk to combine. Slowly drizzle in the olive oil, whisking until thoroughly combined. Add salt to taste.

Lightly dress the tomato and shallot mixture using about 3 to 4 tablespoons of the vinaigrette; be careful not to overdress. To finish the salad, spoon out the dressed tomato mixture onto a plate and top with avocado and the flaked whitefish. Drizzle the tartar with a bit more of the dressing and garnish with a few sprigs of dill and parsley.

TIP To peel the tomatoes, cut a small X into the flesh at the bottom. Drop into boiling water and cook until you can see the skin start to peel back, but for no more than 30 seconds. Cool the tomatoes slightly, and then pull the skin away from the flesh.

Smoked Whitefish Rillettes with Bacon Jam

THIS DISH IS A SHOWSTOPPER for any kind of party, and it goes incredibly well on a thoughtful charcuterie platter. The smokiness of the whitefish and the fatty, salty, smoky nature of the bacon pair beautifully, while the sweetness of the bacon jam helps cut through the richness.

Serves 4–6

¼ cup olive oil
1 pound bacon, sliced into quarter-inch matchsticks
butter
2 medium yellow onions, sliced
1 tablespoon sherry vinegar
6 ounces smoked whitefish, flaked
1 tablespoon finely minced chives for garnish

Add olive oil and bacon to a skillet over medium heat and cook until the bacon is crisp and the fat is fully rendered. Drain bacon on a paper towel–lined plate; pull away excess fat. Drain oil from pan and reserve with extra bacon fat.

Add 1 tablespoon bacon fat, 2 tablespoons butter, and onions to the now-empty skillet and place over medium heat. Cook slowly until the onions are light caramel in color; pour in vinegar and cook, scraping up any browned bits, until pan is nearly dry. Continue cooking until the onions become a deep, rich caramel color, then stir in the cooked bacon. Continue to cook for 3 to 4 minutes, until the bacon is thoroughly incorporated. Remove from skillet and let the mixture cool to room temperature, then place in the refrigerator until needed.

For the rillettes, add the smoked whitefish and ⅔ cup bacon fat to a saucepan over medium to medium-low heat. Bring to a simmer and cook until the fish is soft enough to be smashed with a fork. Remove the fish from the pot and place in a mixing bowl. Smash with a fork until the fish starts to become pasty. Slowly drizzle in the warm bacon fat and whisk to thoroughly combine the fat with the fish. Spoon into a ramekin and let cool to room temperature, then place in the refrigerator until needed.

Garnish the rillettes with the fresh chives and serve with the bacon jam and a variety of your favorite pickled veggies and cured meats for an impromptu charcuterie party.

Whitefish and White Bean Soup

THIS SOUP IS A GREAT way to use up fish scraps. I tend to use leftover bellies, cutting them into small pieces and gently poaching them in the soup just before serving. You could make this soup all year round using whatever kind of veggies you have on hand, but this version is great for a cold winter day.

Serves at least 4

2 tablespoons olive oil
½ red onion, chopped
1 carrot, peeled and cut into quarter-inch pieces
½ fennel bulb, thinly sliced
1 tablespoon sherry vinegar
6 cups chicken stock
1 (15-ounce) can white beans, rinsed and drained
4–6 whitefish bellies, sliced into half-inch pieces

Warm olive oil in a large saucepan over medium heat. Stir in onion and cook until softened and translucent. Stir in carrot and fennel and continue to cook until fennel softens. Add vinegar and cook, scraping up any browned bits, until the vinegar almost completely evaporates. Stir in chicken stock and white beans and simmer until beans are creamy in the center, about 15 to 20 minutes. Add in the chopped fish bellies. Poach until the fish turns white and is cooked through. Season with salt and pepper. Garnish with fennel fronds.

Smoked Whitefish Bisque with Fried Shallots

THE FLAKY FLESH OF LAKE Superior whitefish is ideal for eating, but its hardy nature also means that it holds up well to smoking and curing. This easy-to-make bisque is a perfect spring, fall, or winter dish. If you can't find smoked whitefish, smoked Alaskan salmon is a good, sustainable substitute.

Serves 4

butter
¼ cup chopped carrot
¼ cup chopped celery
½ cup chopped yellow onion
2 tablespoons sherry (optional)
½ cup chopped potato
1 cup heavy cream
2 cups chicken stock
1 sprig fresh thyme
2 cups chopped and deboned smoked whitefish
¼ cup vegetable oil
1 medium shallot, cut into rings
1 tablespoon all-purpose flour
2 tablespoons chopped chives

Melt 2 tablespoons butter in a medium saucepan over medium heat and add carrots, celery, and onions. Cook until vegetables soften and onions start to become translucent. Stir in sherry (if using) and cook, scraping up any browned bits, until it reduces to almost nothing. Stir in potatoes, cream, stock, and thyme. Bring to a simmer and cook until potatoes become fork tender. Add in 1 ½ cups smoked whitefish and simmer for 5 to 10 minutes. After the whitefish has steeped in the broth, remove the sprig of thyme. Carefully add soup to a blender and blend until smooth. Return bisque to the saucepan and keep warm.

In another medium saucepan, heat vegetable oil to 350 degrees. Toss the shallots with the flour, carefully place shallots into the hot oil, and fry until golden brown, about 1 minute. Drain on a paper towel–lined plate and season with salt to taste. Use as a garnish for the bisque, along with fresh chopped chives and the remaining whitefish.

Midwestern Fisherman's Stew

EVERY FISHING CULTURE THROUGHOUT THE world has its own variation on a fisherman's stew. These stews often reflect the rustic nature of the lives of those dedicated to their profession while also offering a unique insight into the region. With this dish, I tried to create a version that reflects the Midwest using bright yet bold flavors and a selection of common fish. Across the globe, each variation of fisherman's stew is designed to use whatever the fisherman brought home that day—and this dish is very much the same. Feel free to use whatever fish is on hand, but try to incorporate at least three varieties to help round out the overall flavor.

Serves at least 4

8 ounces cleaned smelt
8 ounces whitefish fillets (walleye, sunfish, crappie)
8 ounces trout (or freshwater salmon) fillets
olive oil
butter
1 onion, finely chopped
1 carrot, finely chopped
1 rib celery, finely chopped
¼ cup sherry vinegar
1 cup white wine
2 (15-ounce) cans crushed tomatoes
2 cups fish (or chicken) stock
1 tablespoon red chile flakes
¼ cup chopped dill
¼ cup chopped tarragon
pinch saffron (4–6 threads)

Drizzle fish with olive oil and sprinkle with salt. Working in batches, place smelt and fillets on a grill pan over high heat and quickly brown, about 1 to 2 minutes per side. Remove from heat and set aside.

Add 2 tablespoons butter and 2 tablespoons olive oil to a large saucepan over medium-high heat. After the butter has melted, add onions, carrots, and celery and cook until the vegetables begin to soften. Season with salt. Stir in the vinegar and cook until almost completely reduced; stir in white wine and reduce by at least half. Reduce heat to medium and stir in tomatoes, stock, and chile flakes. Simmer until the mixture starts to reduce, about 15 minutes.

Cut fish into about 1-inch pieces. Stir fresh herbs and fish into the stew and simmer for 5 to 10 minutes or until the fish is cooked through and incorporated into the stock. Season with salt and pepper and serve.

Whitefish Ratatouille

THIS HEARTY DISH IS ACTUALLY perfect all year round: just use a variety of seasonal vegetables to round out the mix. The fish helps keep the dish on the lighter side of things, and while I opted to use Lake Superior whitefish, you could choose any white flaky fish. Roast the fish and either serve it as a fillet on top of the ratatouille or flake it into the mixture, which is what I like to do. A fried egg on top adds richness and depth—and, really, when does adding a fried egg ever hurt?

Serves 2–4

olive oil
½ red onion, sliced
1 red bell pepper, chopped
1 yellow bell pepper, chopped
2 cups chopped eggplant
2 tablespoons white wine
1 (24-ounce) can crushed tomatoes
1 tablespoon red chile flakes
butter
4 (4- to 6-ounce) whitefish fillets
4 large fresh eggs
chopped parsley, for garnish

For the ratatouille, heat 2 tablespoons olive oil in a skillet over medium-high heat. Add the onions and cook until translucent. Stir in red peppers, yellow peppers, and eggplant and season with a pinch of salt. Continue to cook until the vegetables start to soften. Stir in white wine and cook, scraping up any browned bits, until mostly evaporated. Stir in crushed tomatoes and chile flakes, reduce heat to medium low, and simmer until the sauce reduces to a thick ragu.

For the fish, add 1 tablespoon olive oil and 1 tablespoon butter to a skillet on medium-high heat. Pat fillets dry and season with salt. Place fillets in skillet and cook two-thirds of the way through on one side, about 2 to 3 minutes. Flip and cook for an additional 1 to 2 minutes or until the fish is cooked through and flaky.

For the eggs, heat 1 tablespoon olive oil and 1 tablespoon butter in a skillet over medium heat. When the pan is hot, crack in eggs and fry until desired doneness. I recommend sunny side up or over easy.

To finish, either flake the fish into the ratatouille and spoon into a bowl, or scoop the ratatouille into a bowl and top with the fillets. Add finished egg and garnish with parsley.

Whitefish and Collard Greens with Mustard Vinaigrette

THIS PRETTY RUSTIC DISH IS completely satisfying. Serve with roasted potatoes or even some nice creamy grits.

Serves 4

1 tablespoon mustard
4 tablespoons cider vinegar
1 tablespoon chopped capers
olive oil
4 slices bacon, sliced into quarter-inch matchsticks
1 shallot, chopped
1 bunch collard greens, chopped (about 4 cups)
zest of ½ lemon
1 tablespoon red chile flakes
½ cup chicken stock
4 (4- to 6-ounce) whitefish fillets
butter

Add mustard and 2 tablespoons vinegar to a small mixing bowl, whisking to combine. Stir in the capers and slowly drizzle in 6 tablespoons olive oil, whisking until the vinaigrette comes together. Season with salt and pepper and refrigerate until needed.

Add bacon to a cold skillet and place on medium-high heat. As the fat renders out and the bacon starts to brown, add in the shallots. Once the shallots become soft and translucent, stir in collard greens. As the collards start to wilt and decrease in volume, stir in remaining 2 tablespoons vinegar and cook, scraping up any browned bits, until the vinegar has almost entirely evaporated. Stir in lemon zest, chile flakes, and chicken stock. Heat until the chicken stock comes up to a simmer, then cover and reduce heat to medium low. Simmer until the collards are tender, about 20 minutes.

Pat fish dry and season with salt. Add 1 tablespoon butter and 1 tablespoon olive oil to a pan over medium heat. Once butter melts and becomes frothy, add in fish and cook on one side until two-thirds done, 2 to 3 minutes, then flip and cook for an additional 1 to 2 minutes or until the fish is cooked through and flaky. Serve the fish atop the collard greens and dress with the vinaigrette.

Smoked Cisco on Toast (page 51)

INDEX

A

aioli
Grilled Northern with Fried Artichokes and Lemon-Tarragon Aioli, 89
Sunfish Arancini with Lemon Aioli, 156
appetizers
Bass Spring Rolls, 15
Cisco on Toast, 51
Northern Eggrolls, 79
Pan-Fried Smelt with Garlic Chips, Lemon, Parsley, and Olive Oil, 135
Perch Cocktail, 106
Smelt in Sofrito, 132
Sunfish Pot Stickers, 141
Trout-Stuffed Mushrooms, 180
Walleye Cakes, 196
Walleye Lettuce Wraps, 187
apples
Grilled Northern with Apple and Green Onion Refried Farro, 102
Roasted Crappie with Apple-Brussels Hash and Cider Crème, 71
Walleye Waldorf, 188
artichokes
Grilled Northern with Fried Artichokes and Lemon-Tarragon Aioli, 89
asparagus
Grilled Perch with Mushroom Broth and Fiddlehead Ferns, 124
Perch with Asparagus Sauce, Roasted Asparagus Tips, and Pickled Shallot, 116
Sunfish and Asparagus Risotto, 154
Sunfish Arancini with Lemon Aioli, 156
Trout-Stuffed Mushrooms with Baked Eggs, 180
avocado
Tomato Tartare with Dill and Parsley Vinaigrette, Smoked Whitefish, and Avocado, 206

B

bacon
Buffalo Bass with Celery, Blue Cheese, and Bacon Salad, 19
Catfish and Bacon Benedicts, 39
Crappie Schnitzel, Brown Butter and Bacon Spaetzle, and Braised Red Cabbage, 70
Northern BLTs, 82
Northern with Pan-Roasted Balsamic Grapes, 99
Roasted Crappie with Apple-Brussles Hash and Cider Cream, 71
Smoked Whitefish Rillettes with Bacon Jam, 209
Sunfish Hash, 159
Trout Quiche with Bacon and Leeks, 179
Whitefish and Collard Greens with Mustard Vinaigrette, 216
barbecue
BBQ Northern with Cajun Fried Rice, 96
bass: 14–31
Bass and Mushroom Noodle Soup, 16
Bass au Poivre, 25
Bass Spring Rolls, 15
Bass with Warm Carrot Salad, 18
Beer Battered Bass Fish and Chips, 20
Buffalo Bass with Celery, Blue Cheese, and Bacon Salad, 19
Crispy Bass and Basil Stir-Fry, 23
Grilled Bass with White Pesto, 28
Salt-Crusted Bass with Chive Hollandaise, 31
Whole Grilled Bass with Citrus Chimichurri, 26
beans, green
Rainbow Trout Niçoise, 164
Trout Amandine, 176
beans, red or black or white
Blackened Crappie with Red Beans and Rice, 73
Crappie Enchiladas, 67
Trout, Corn, and Black Bean Salad, 168
Whitefish and White Bean Soup, 211
beer
Beer Battered Bass Fish and Chips, 20
Northern Pike Nuggets with Tartar Sauce, 76
Perch Tacos, 110
beets
Smoked Trout and Pickled Yellow Beet Salad with Crème Fraîche, 167
Benedicts
Catfish and Bacon Benedicts, 39
blackened
Blackened Crappie with Red Beans and Rice, 73
blue cheese
Buffalo Bass with Celery, Blue Cheese, and Bacon Salad, 19
breakfast
Catfish and Bacon Benedicts, 39
Catfish and Chipotle Johnnycakes, 34
Soft Scrambled Eggs with Cisco Roe, 52
Spanish Tortilla with Roasted Red Peppers, 182
Sunfish Hash, 159
Trout Quiche with Bacon and Leeks, 179
Trout-Stuffed Mushrooms with Baked Eggs, 180
brunch. *See* breakfast; lunch
Brussels sprouts
Roasted Crappie with Apple-Brussels Hash and Cider Cream, 71
burgers
Green Onion and Dill Northern Burgers, 84

C

Cajun
BBQ Northern with Cajun Fried Rice, 96
Blackened Crappie with Red Beans and Rice, 73
Catfish and Bacon Benedicts, 39

3ass Spring
Rolls (page 15)

Crispy Roasted Sunfish with Braised Endive, Cauliflower Puree, and Orange Sauce (page 145)

carrots
Bass with Warm Carrot Salad, 18
Cisco Escabeche with Fennel and Carrot, 61
Pan-Roasted Pike with Roasted Carrots and Honey-Vinegar Glaze, 86
catfish: 32–47
Catfish and Bacon Benedicts, 39
Catfish and Chipotle Johnnycakes, 34
Catfish Gumbo, 34
Cornmeal-Crusted Catfish with Charred Kale and Tomato, Corn, and Chipotle Salsa, 40
Grilled Catfish with Thai-Inspired Vinaigrette, 43
Indian-Style Roasted Catfish with Cucumber Yogurt Sauce, 46
Pecan-Crusted Catfish with Honey Mustard Sauce, 44
cauliflower
Crispy Roasted Sunfish with Braised Endive, Cauliflower Puree, and Orange Sauce, 145
Grilled Bass with White Pesto, 28
celariac
Pan-Roasted Rainbow Trout with Oven-Roasted Mushrooms, Celeriac Puree, and Red Wine Sauce, 172
chimichurri
Whole Grilled Bass with Citrus Chimichurri, 26
Chinese (cuisine), 79
chipotles
Catfish and Chipotle Johnnycakes, 34
Cornmeal-Crusted Catfish with Charred Kale and Tomato, Corn, and Chipotle Salsa, 40
Crappie Enchiladas, 67
Perch Corndogs with Spicy Rhubarb Ketchup, 108
Perch Tacos, 110
cisco: 50–61
Cisco Escabeche with Fennel and Carrot, 61
Cisco Rice Bowl with Spicy Mayo, 58
Grilled Cisco with Pickled Green Tomato and Pistachio Salad, 57
Smoked Cisco and Herb Salad, 54
Smoked Cisco on Toast, 51
Soft Scrambled Eggs with Cisco Roe, 52
citrus
Grilled Northern with Fennel and Citrus Salad, 100
Oven-Roasted Sunfish, Fennel, and Orange with Potato Puree and Chile Citrus Beurre Blanc, 147
Whole Grilled Bass with Citrus Chimichurri, 26
collard greens
Whitefish and Collard Greens with Mustard Vinaigrette, 216
commercial food industry, 4
corn
Catfish and Chipotle Johnnycakes, 34
Cornmeal-Crusted Catfish with Charred Kale and Tomato, Corn, and Chipotle Salsa, 40
Grilled Walleye Succotash, 200
Trout, Corn, and Black Bean Salad, 168
cornmeal
Catfish and Chipotle Johnnycakes, 34
Cornmeal-Crusted Catfish with Charred Kale and Tomato, Corn, and Chipotle Salsa, 40
Perch Corndogs with Spicy Rhubarb Ketchup, 108
crappie: 64–73
Blackened Crappie with Red Beans and Rice, 71
Crappie Enchiladas, 67
Crappie Pie, 67
Crappie Rachel, 66
Crappie Schnitzel, Brown Butter and Bacon Spaetzle, and Braised Red Cabbage, 70
Fried Crappie Pajeon, 64
Roasted Crappie with Apple-Brussels Hash and Cider Cream, 71
cucumbers
Bass Spring Rolls, 15
Cisco Rice Bowl with Spicy Mayo, 58
Grilled Northern Pike with Fresh Summer Gazpacho, 81
Grilled Perch with Cucumber Mignonette, 123
Grilled Perch with Eggplant and Tzatziki, 121
Indian-Style Roasted Catfish with Cucumber Yogurt Sauce, 46
Perch Flatbread, 109
Trout with Cucumber Salad, 171

D

Department of Natural Resources, Minnesota, 6, 7, 8
dill
Green Onion and Dill Northern Burgers, 84
Grilled Northern and Zucchini with Herbed Vinaigrette, 85
Grilled Northern Pike with Fresh Summer Gazpacho, 81
Midwestern Fisherman's Stew, 213
Pan-Roasted Pike with Roasted Carrots and Honey-Vinegar Glaze, 86
Perch Flatbreads, 109
Smoked Cisco and Herb Salad, 54
Smoked Cisco on Toast, 51
Smoked Trout and Pickled Yellow Beet Salad with Crème Fraîche, 167
Sunfish and Shells with Dill Cream, 158
Tomato Tartare with Dill and Parsley Vinaigrette, Smoked Whitefish, and Avocado, 206

E

egg(s)
Catfish and Bacon Benedicts, 39
Soft Scrambled Eggs with Cisco Roe, 52
Spanish Trout Tortilla with Roasted Red Peppers, 182
Trout Quiche with Bacon and Leeks, 179
Trout-Stuffed Mushrooms with Baked Eggs, 180
enchiladas
Crappie Enchilada, 67
endive
Crispy Roasted Sunfish with Braised Endive, Cauliflower Puree, and Orange Sauce, 145

escabeche
Cisco Escabeche with Fennel and Carrot, 61

F

farm-raised fish, 5, 9, 10
farro
Grilled Northern with Apple and Green Onion Refried Farro, 102
fennel
Cisco Escabeche with Fennel and Carrot, 61
Grilled Northern with Fennel and Citrus Salad, 100
Oven-Roasted Sunfish, Fennel, and Orange with Potato Puree and Chile Citrus Beuree Blanc, 147
Whitefish and White Bean Soup, 211
fiddlehead ferns
Grilled Perch with Mushroom Broth and Fiddlehead Ferns, 124
fish. *See also* specific species
hatcheries, 9
processing of, industrial, 9
stocks, in Minnesota, 7
fish and chips
Beer Battered Bass Fish and Chips, 20
fish cakes
Catfish and Chipotle Johnnycakes, 34
Fried Crappie Pajeon, 64
Walleye Cakes, 196
fish tacos
Grilled Walleye Tacos with Mango Salsa, 194
Perch Tacos, 110
fishing
commercial, 6, 7, 8
sport, 3, 4, 6, 8, 9
subsistence, 6

G

gazpacho
Grilled Northern Pike with Fresh Summer Gazpacho, 81
grapes
Northern with Pan-Roasted Balsamic Grapes, 99
gumbo
Catfish Gumbo, 37

H

harissa
Bass with Warm Carrot Salad, 18
Harissa Grilled Smelt with Mint and Cilantro Yogurt, 128
hollandaise
Catfish and Bacon Benedicts, 39
Salt-Crusted Bass with Chive Hollandaise, 31

I

Indian (cuisine), 46
Italian (cuisine), 57, 96, 121, 202

J

Japanese (cuisine), 58
johnnycakes
Catfish and Chiptole Johnnycakes, 34

K

kale
Cornmeal-Crusted Catfish with Charred Kale and Tomato, Corn, and Chipotle Salsa, 40
Smoked Trout Kale Niçoise, 165
ketchup
Beer Battered Bass Fish and Chips, 20
Crappie Rachel, 66
Perch Cocktail, 106
Perch Corndogs with Spicy Rhubarb Ketchup, 108
kimchi
Sunfish and Kimchi Fried Rice, 153
Korean (cuisine), 64

L

Lake Superior
as fishery, 6–7, 10
Smelt in Sofrito, 132
Smoked Whitefish Bisque with Fried Shallots, 212
Soft Scrambled Eggs with Cisco Roe, 52
Whitefish Ratatouille, 215
lakes
as food source, 4, 7, 9
for recreation, 3, 6, 9
leeks
Crappie Pie, 68
Trout Quiche with Bacon and Leeks, 179
lunch
Cisco Escabeche with Fennel and Carrot, 61
Perch Flatbreads, 109
Smoked Cisco on Toast, 51
Sunfish Sandwich, 142

M

main dishes
Bass and Mushroom Noodle Soup, 16
Buffalo Bass with Celery, Blue Cheese, and Bacon Salad, 19
Cisco Escabeche with Fennel and Carrot, 61
Cornmeal-Crusted Catfish with Charred Kale and Tomato, Corn, and Chipotle Salsa, 40
Crispy Roasted Sunfish with Braised Endive, Cauliflower Puree, and Orange Sauce, 145
Grilled Northern and Zucchini with Herbed Vinaigrette, 85
Grilled Northern with Fried Artichokes and Lemon-Tarragon Aioli, 89
Grilled Walleye Succotash, 200

atfish and Chipotle Johnnycakes (page 34)

Perch Flatbreads (page 109)

Grilled Walleye Tacos with Mango Salsa, 194
Grilled Walleye with Grilled Apricot and Herb Salad, 191
Northern Pike Nuggets with Tartar Sauce, 76
Northern with Pan-Roasted Balsamic Grapes, 99
Pan-Roasted Pike with Roasted Carrots and Honey-Vinegar Glaze, 86
Pasta al Luccio, 202
Perch with Asparagus Sauce, Roasted Asparagus Tips, and Pickled Shallots, 116
Red Wine Poached Trout, 175
Seared Northern with Mushrooms, Onions, and Beurre Rouge, 91
Trout Amandine, 176
Walleye Basil Stir-Fry, 198
Walleye with Morels and Brown Butter, 197
Whitefish and Collard Greens with Mustard Vinaigrette, 216
Whitefish Ratatouille, 215
Whole Grilled Bass with Citrus Chimichurri, 26
mango
Grilled Walleye Tacos with Mango Salsa, 194
Mediterranean (cuisine), 61, 121
Minnesota, commercial fishing in, 6, 7, 8
Monterey Bay Aquarium, 5. *See also* Seafood Watch
Moroccan (cuisine), 18
mushrooms
Bass and Mushroom Noodle Soup, 16
Grilled Perch with Mushroom Broth and Fiddlehead Ferns, 124
Pan-Roasted Rainbow Trout with Oven-Roasted Mushrooms, Celeriac Puree, and Red Wine Sauce, 172
Seared Northern with Mushrooms, Onions, and Beurre Rouge, 91
Trout-Stuffed Mushrooms with Baked Eggs, 180
Walleye with Morels and Brown Butter, 197

N

niçoise
Rainbow Trout Niçoise, 164
Smoked Trout Kale Niçoise, 165
noodles
Bass and Mushroom Noodle Soup, 16
Bass Spring Rolls, 15
Pasta al Luccio, 202
Sunfish and Shells with Dill Cream, 158
northern pike: 76–103
BBQ Northern with Cajun Fried Rice, 96
Green Onion and Dill Northern Burgers, 84
Grilled Northern and Zucchini with Herbed Vinaigrette, 85
Grilled Northern Pike with Fresh Summer Gazpacho, 81
Grilled Northern with Apple and Green Onion Refried Farro, 102
Grilled Northern with Fennel and Citrus Salad, 100
Grilled Northern with Fried Artichokes and Lemon-Tarragon Aioli, 89
Grilled Northern with Romesco Sauce, 92
Grilled Northern with Sauce Vierge, 95
Northern BLTs, 82
Northern Eggrolls, 79
Northern Pike Nuggets with Tartar Sauce, 76
Northern with Pan-Roasted Balsamic Grapes, 99
Pan-Roasted Pike with Roasted Carrots and Honey-Vinegar Glaze, 86
Seared Northern with Mushrooms, Onions, and Beurre Rouge, 91

O

ocean fish, 4, 5, 9. *See also* seafood
overfishing, 7, 10

P

paella
Sunfish Paella, 150
pajeon
Fried Crappie Pajeon, 64
pasta
Pasta Al Luccio, 202
Sunfish with Shells and Dill Cream, 158
perch: 106–25
Broiled Perch with Ramp Salsa Verde and Wild Rice, 113
Grilled Perch with Cucumber Mignonette, 123
Grilled Perch with Eggplant and Tzatziki, 121
Grilled Perch with Mushroom Broth and Fiddlehead Ferns, 123
Perch Cocktail, 106
Perch Corndogs with Spicy Rhubarb Ketchup, 108
Perch Flatbreads, 109
Perch Tacos, 110
Perch with Asparagus Sauce, Roasted Asparagus Tips, and Pickled Shallot, 115
Roasted Perch with Sautéed Radishes and Radish-Top Pesto, 115
Seared Perch with Caramelized Butternut Squash and Balsamic, 118
pesto
Grilled Bass with White Pesto, 28
Roasted Perch with Sautéed Radishes and Radish-Top Pesto, 115
pickles
Hot Fried Sunnies with Pickled Onion and Chile Mayo, 148
Perch with Asparagus Sauce, Roasted Asparagus Tips, and Pickled Shallots, 116
Smoked Trout and Pickled Yellow Beet Salad with Crème Fraîche, 167
pot stickers
Sunfish Pot Stickers, 141
potatoes
Beer Battered Bass Fish and Chips, 20
Oven-Roasted Sunfish, Fennel, and Orange with Potato Puree and Chile Citrus Beurre Blanc, 147

Rainbow Trout Niçoise, 164
Smoked Trout Kale Niçoise, 165
Smoked Whitefish Bisque with Fried Shallots, 212
Spanish Trout Tortilla with Roasted Red Peppers, 182
Sunfish Hash, 159
Trout Amandine, 176

Q

quiche
Spanish Trout Tortilla with Roasted Red Peppers, 182
Trout Quiche with Bacon and Leeks, 179

R

radishes
Cisco Rice Bowl with Spicy Mayo, 58
Crappie Enchiladas, 67
Perch Cocktail, 106
Roasted Perch with Sautéed Radishes and Radish-Top Pesto, 115
Smoked Cisco and Herb Salad, 54
Smoked Trout and Pickled Yellow Beet Salad with Crème Fraîche, 167
ramps
Broiled Perch with Ramp Salsa Verde and Wild Rice, 113
Walleye with Morels and Brown Butter, 197
ratatouille
Whitefish Ratatouille, 215
Red Lake (Minnesota), 10
rhubarb
Perch Corn Dogs with Spicy Rhubarb Ketchup, 108
rillettes
Smoked Whitefish Rillettes with Bacon Jam, 209
risotto
Sunfish and Asparagus Risotto, 154
Sunfish Arancini with Lemon Aioli, 156
roe
Soft Scrambled Eggs with Cisco Roe, 52

S

salads
Bass with Warm Carrot Salad, 18
Grilled Smelt Caeser Salad, 137
Rainbow Trout Niçoise, 164
Smoked Cisco and Herb Salad, 54
Smoked Trout and Pickled Yellow Beet Salad with Crème Fraîche, 167
Smoked Trout Kale Niçoise, 165
Trout, Corn, and Black Bean Salad, 168
Walleye Waldorf, 188
salsa
Broiled Perch with Ramp Salsa Verde and Wild Rice, 113
Catfish and Chipotle Johnnycakes, 34
Cornmeal-Crusted Catfish with Charred Kale and Tomato, Corn, and Chipotle Salsa, 40
Crappie Enchiladas, 67
Grilled Walleye Tacos with Mango Salsa, 194
salt crust
Salt-Crusted Bass with Chive Hollandaise, 31
sandwiches
Classic Minnesota-Style Walleye Sandwich, 193
Crappie Rachel, 66
Green Onion and Dill Northern Burgers, 84
Northern BLTs, 82
Sunfish Sandwich, 142
Trout Tartine, 162
sauces
Bass au Poivre, 25
Bass Spring Rolls, with peanut, 15
Catfish and Bacon Benedicts, with hollandaise, 39
Crispy Roasted Sunfish with Braised Endive, Cauliflower Puree, and Orange Sauce, 145
Grilled Bass with White Pesto, 28
Grilled Catfish with Thai-Inspired Vinaigrette, 43
Grilled Northern and Zucchini with Herbed Vinaigrette, 85
Grilled Northern with Romesco Sauce, 92
Grilled Northern with Sauce Vierge, 95
Grilled Perch with Cucumber Mignonette, 123
Grilled Perch with Eggplant and Tzatziki, 121
Indian-Style Roasted Catfish with Cucumber Yogurt Sauce, 46
Northern Pike Nuggets with Tartar Sauce, 76
Oven-Roasted Sunfish, Fennel, and Orange with Potato Puree and Chile Citrus Beurre Blanc, 147
Pan-Roasted Pike with Roasted Carrots and Honey-Vinegar Glaze, 86
Pan-Roasted Rainbow Trout with Oven-Roasted Mushrooms, Celeriac Puree, and Red Wine Sauce, 172
Pasta al Luccio, 202
Pecan-Crusted Catfish with Honey Mustard Sauce, 44
Perch with Asparagus Sauce, Roasted Asparagus Tips, and Pickled Shallots, 116
Rainbow Trout Niçoise, with vinaigrette, 164
Roasted Crappie with Apple-Brussles Hash and Cider Cream, 71
Roasted Perch with Sautéed Radishes and Radish-Top Pesto, 115
Salt-Crusted Bass with Chive Hollandaise, 31
Seared Northern with Mushrooms, Onions, and Beurre Rouge, 91
Smoked Cisco and Herb Salad, with vinaigrette, 54
Smoked Cisco on Toast, with creamy mustard sauce, 51
Sunfish and Shells with Dill Cream, 158
Tempura Smelt with Asian-Style Dipping Sauce, 131
Tomato Tartare with Dill and Parsley Vinaigrette, Smoked Whitefish, and Avocado, 206
Whitefish and Collard Greens with Mustard Vinaigrette, 216
Scandinavian (cuisine), 6, 171
schnitzel
Crappie Schnitzel, Brown Butter and Bacon Spaetzle, and Braised Red Cabbage, 70

‑illed Northern with
›mesco Sauce (page 92)

Classic Minnesota-Style Walleye Sandwich (page 193)

seafood, 4, 5–6, 8
Seafood Watch, 5, 10
smelt: 128–37
Grilled Smelt Caeser Salad, 137
Harrissa Grilled Smelt with Mint and Cilantro Yogurt, 127
Pan-Fried Smelt with Garlic Chips, Lemon, Parsley, and Olive Oil, 135
Smelt in Sofrito, 132
Tempura Smelt with Asian-Style Dipping Sauce, 131
soups
Grilled Northern Pike with Fresh Summer Gazpacho, 81
Whitefish and White Bean Soup, 211
Spanish (cuisine), 92, 132, 150, 182
spring rolls
Bass Spring Rolls, 15
squash
Pan-Fried Perch with Caramelized Butternut Squash and Balsamic, 118
succotash
Grilled Walleye Succotash, 200
sunfish: 140–59
Crispy Roasted Sunfish with Braised Endive, Cauliflower Puree, and Orange Sauce, 145
Hot Fried Sunnies with Pickled Onion and Chile Mayo, 148
Oven-Roasted Sunfish, Fennel, and Orange with Potato Puree and Chile Citrus Beurre Blanc, 147
Sunfish and Asparagus Risotto, 154
Sunfish and Kimchi Fried Rice, 153
Sunfish and Shells with Dill Cream, 158
Sunfish Arancini with Lemon Aioli, 156
Sunfish Hash, 159
Sunfish Paella, 150
Sunfish Pot Stickers, 141
Sunfish Sandwich, 142

T

tartar sauce
Beer Battered Bass Fish and Chips, 20
Northern Pike Nuggets with Tartar Sauce, 76
Thai (cuisine), 15, 16, 23, 43, 116, 198
trout: 162–83
Pan Roasted Rainbow Trout with Oven Roasted Mushrooms, Celeriac Puree, and Red Wine Sauce, 172
Rainbow Trout Niçoise, 164
Red Wine Poached Trout, 175
Smoked Trout and Pickled Yellow Beet Salad with Crème Fraîche, 167
Smoked Trout Kale Niçoise, 165
Spanish Trout Tortilla with Roasted Red Peppers, 182
Steamed Trout with Ginger and Green Onions, 172
Trout, Corn, and Black Bean Salad, 167
Trout Amandine, 176
Trout Quiche with Bacon and Leeks, 179
Trout-Stuffed Mushrooms with Baked Eggs, 180
Trout Tartine, 162
Trout with Cucumber Salad, 171

V

vinaigrettes. *See* sauces

W

walleye: 186–203
Classic Minnesota-Style Walleye Sandwich, 193
Grilled Walleye Succotash, 200
Grilled Walleye Tacos with Mango Salsa, 194
Grilled Walleye with Grilled Apricot and Herb Salad, 191
Pasta al Luccio, 202
Walleye Basil Stir-Fry, 198
Walleye Cakes, 196
Walleye Lettuce Wraps, 187
Walleye Waldorf, 188
Walleye with Morels and Brown Butter, 197
whitefish: 206–17
Midwestern Fisherman's Stew, 212
Smoked Whitefish Bisque with Fried Shallots, 211
Smoked Whitefish Rillettes, 209
Tomato Tartare with Dill and Parsley Vinaigrette, Smoked Whitefish, and Avocado, 206
Whitefish and Collard Greens with Mustard Vinaigrette, 216
Whitefish and White Bean Soup, 211
Whitefish Ratatouille, 215
wild rice
Broiled Perch with Ramp Salsa Verde and Wild Rice, 113

Y

yogurt
Grilled Perch with Eggplant and Tzatziki, 121
Harrissa Grilled Smelt with Mint and Cilantro Yogurt, 128
Indian-Style Roasted Catfish with Cucumber Yogurt Sauce, 46

Z

zucchini
Grilled Northern and Zucchini with Herbed Vinaigrette, 85

Lake Fish was designed and set in type by Susan Everson in St. Paul, Minnesota. The typefaces are Alehouse Sans and FreightSans Pro. The book was printed by Versa Press Inc. in East Peoria, Illinois.